SCIENCE

COURSEWORK COMPANION

Bob McDuell

Letts

GCSE

Charles Letts & Co Ltd
London, Edinburgh & New York

First published 1989
by Charles Letts & Co Ltd
Diary House, Borough Road, London SE1 1DW

Text: © Bob McDuell 1989
Illustrations: © Charles Letts & Co Ltd 1989
Cover photograph: Steven Hunt, Image Bank
Handwriting samples: Artistic License
Diagrams: Ian Foulis and Associates
Cartoons: Kate Charlesworth
Photograph on page 93: Ohaus UK Ltd

All our Rights Reserved. No part of this
publication may be reproduced, stored in a retrieval
system, or transmitted, in any form
or by any means, electronic, mechanical,
photocopying, recording or otherwise, without the
prior permission of Charles Letts Publishers.

'Letts' is a registered trademark of
Charles Letts (Scotland) Ltd

British Library Cataloguing in Publication Data

McDuell, G.R. (Godfrey Robert, *1944*-
  GCSE science
  1. Science–For schools
  I. Title
  500

ISBN 0 85097 863 7

Printed and bound in Great Britain by
Charles Letts (Scotland) Ltd

Contents

	Page
Preface	4
Section one – Introduction	5
Guide to using this book	5
Section two – Why coursework?	6
Section three – How to get the best marks in coursework	7
Section four – Skills to be assessed in practical assessments	8
National criteria	8
Skills	8
Section five – Questions to develop practical skills	22
Section six – Answers to questions	63
Appendix 1 – Examination groups: addresses	88
Appendix 2 – Common apparatus	89

Preface

Letts Revise Series provide excellent preparation for students preparing for science, physics, chemistry and biology GCSE examinations. They concentrate on all aspects of the written examinations. However, all GCSE examinations in the sciences now include compulsory coursework which includes an assessment of practical skills. This can account for 25 per cent of the total mark and can make quite a difference to the overall grade awarded. This book is designed to complement the Letts Revise Series and provide help to students to develop and improve performance in practical assessments whether in science or the separate sciences.

The help arises from my experience as a teacher, as a designer of coursework schemes for different examination groups and as a Senior Coursework Assessor.

In writing this book I have enlisted the support and experience of other teachers, examiners and assessors, including Jackie Callaghan-Martin. I would like to thank the staff of Charles Letts Books. Finally, I would like to thank my wife, Judy, and my sons, Robin and Timothy, for help given and for patience during my long spells on the word processor.

Bob McDuell 1989

SECTION ONE

Introduction

Guide to using this book

This book is designed to help you to get your best marks in coursework, especially in practical assessments. The book is suitable for you if you are studying for science or for the separate sciences: physics, chemistry and biology.

It is important to find out from your teacher or from the examination syllabus exactly what is required by way of coursework assessments. Find out which skills are to be assessed and use this book to help you to improve in these skill areas. Usually your teacher will tell you when you are being assessed and what skills he or she is assessing. These practical assessments can be carried out as part of ordinary lessons or they could be organized at special times.

In this book you will find a list of the skills which are usually assessed and advice to help you to do your best in each of them. Then you will find a large number of questions which will help you to develop and improve these skills. If you work carefully through the questions which are appropriate for the subject you are taking, you can then compare your answers with the sample answers given. You should find that, with practice, your answers get better, showing that you are improving in these skill areas.

To help you there is a coding system for subject areas and for skills being used.

For subject areas

⟨S⟩ suitable for science GCSE courses

⟨P⟩ suitable for physics GCSE courses

⟨C⟩ suitable for chemistry GCSE courses

⟨B⟩ suitable for biology GCSE courses

So if you see

⟨S⟩ ⟨B⟩

before a question, it means the question is suitable for science and biology GCSE courses.

For the skills being tested

(a) following instructions
(b) selecting and using apparatus safely
(c) making accurate observations and measurements
(d) recording accurately
(e) drawing conclusions from results
(f) planning simple experiments, testing hypotheses and problem solving
(g) suggesting improvements to experiments.

SECTION TWO

Why coursework?

All GCSE courses contain some element of coursework. This varies from subject to subject and syllabus to syllabus. The idea is that the conscientious student should be able to carry marks forward from work done *during* the course and the final result should not depend *solely* on the work done in one or two examination papers.

In science subjects the most essential element is the **practical assessment**. During your science lessons you will carry out different experiments and your teacher will assess the work that you have done. Your teacher will have planned exercises which enable you to demonstrate your abilities in practical work. Your work will have been marked by your teacher. Usually only your *best* marks in each of the skills areas will be counted. Samples of work from your school or college are usually sent to an **assessor** who will make sure that the standard of marking and the type of exercise used compare fairly with those used for students in other centres.

Although this assessment is of practical skills *in the laboratory*, there is a great deal that you can do in preparation for practical assessments *at home*.

SECTION THREE

How to get the best marks in coursework

Students often worry about the coursework for GCSE. Part of the problem is caused by clashes caused by coursework in different subjects causing pressure at certain times of the course. Coursework in sciences in the form of practical assessment usually takes place in your laboratory during timetabled lessons. There should not be a lot of work to take home from this.

It is important to remember that the practical assessment is *not* designed for some candidates to fail. All candidates should do well. Obviously some candidates will do better than others. An experienced assessor of practical assessments might well expect the majority of candidates in a good school or college to get marks between 18 and 25 out of 25 overall. A number of candidates having full marks is *not* unusual. This is to be *expected*, especially when a selection is made of a student's *best* marks.

Make sure you have completed enough assessments. Often, because of illness or other reasons, a student's practical assessment is not complete. Check with your teachers well in advance and if necessary seek their cooperation in completing enough assessments.

Treat every assessment exercise just like an ordinary lesson. Do not get uptight if the practical appears to go wrong. Remember that you have only got to complete a limited number of assessments and *everybody's* experiments go wrong at times – just ask your teachers!

Listen to the advice that your teacher gives you about experiments and about your performance of them. He or she will give you good advice which you can act upon. Do not be afraid to ask for help. Students are often afraid to ask because they believe they will incur a penalty by asking. It may be worth risking a penalty to get the vital piece of information to complete an exercise successfully and safely.

Often, especially if you are in a large class, you will work in groups of perhaps two or three. Your teacher has to complete the assessment on the basis of the work that *you* do. However, during the two year course you will have the opportunity of working many times in a group. It is often possible to learn from others in the group. Sharing ideas and developing ideas together is very much how progress is made in the real world in science and other fields.

Your teacher may keep all of your practical assessments for you or, alternatively, expect you to keep them and produce them if they are required by the assessor. If you are entrusted with them, make sure they are kept safely in a file or large cardboard envelope folder. Remember, they **must not be destroyed** when the GCSE examination is finished. If you ultimately decide to resit the examination your practical assessment will be re-submitted. However, you *will* have the opportunity of adding to it and improving it.

Finally, make sure that you present your work well. Poor presentation is not marked down but, if your work is required by the assessor, it helps him or her to help you if your work is clear and well-written. Make sure every piece of work is clearly dated and titled.

> *'Teachers sometimes use a system of 'cue cards'. If you need help you can ask for a cue card, which will help you but will reduce the maximum mark you can obtain. Cue cards can be particularly useful with planning exercises. They may get you started along the right lines.'*

SECTION FOUR

Skills to be assessed in practical assessments

National criteria

The skills which may be assessed come from the **national criteria** in science and separate sciences. These were devised to give 'common ground' for the development of syllabuses.

The same skills appear in all of the syllabuses. Sometimes they are packaged together in different ways. An analysis of the different skills that are tested in questions is given on page 22.

Skills

For the purpose of this book and to fit the widest number of individual assessment schemes, the skills in which you will be assessed have been divided into seven areas, labelled **(a) – (g)**.

(a) Following instructions

It is difficult in a book of this type to help you to improve this skill. However, of all the skills, this is the one you should have least difficulty with. Having followed a GCSE course for at least two years and having completed nearly five years of science in secondary schools, you should be good at following the instructions you are given. These are probably given to you in the form of written instructions and/or diagrams on a sheet of paper. The instructions have been designed to be easy to follow.

Read the instructions through *carefully* from beginning to end. Make sure you understand the **aim** of the experiment. If you do not, read them through again. Next, read them once more and identify the **practical steps** you have to follow. It is a good idea at this stage to mark these with a 'highlighter' pen. (Check with your teacher first. Sometimes he or she may wish to re-use the sheets. If you ask nicely, though, it will probably be all right!) Then, as you work through the instructions, **check** that you have completed everything that you highlighted.

The marks obtained for following instructions are usually high. It is something that most students will be able to do well.

> *Before starting an experiment, check the instructions to make sure you have all the equipment you need. Check it is working properly and you know how to use it.*

(b) Selecting and using apparatus safely

This is an important skill which we can develop well. It is important to know how to use a wide range of apparatus. The choice of suitable apparatus and using it safely is important in itself. However, when you get onto skills **(f)** and **(g)**, requiring planning of investigations, it is important to know what possibilities exist. Many students fail to achieve high marks in planning because they do not understand what apparatus can be used for. Appendix 2 includes information about common apparatus and we shall consider it under several headings:

- general laboratory glass and china ware
- other items of general apparatus
- the Bunsen burner
- weighing equipment
- thermometers
- electrical apparatus
- microscopes
- centrifuge

Safety in the laboratory

Figure 4.1 shows a general view of a laboratory where there are several possible causes of accidents to be seen. List the possible causes of accidents and compare your list with the list on page 21.

Fig. 4.1 Safety in the laboratory?

Figure 4.2 shows a number of laboratory situations where common mistakes are being made. Decide in each case what the person is doing wrong.

Fig. 4.2 Safety in the laboratory!

> *If you do not know how to use a piece of apparatus safely, ask your teacher.*

> *When using apparatus, check that it is clean before you use it. If in doubt, wash it.*

(c) Making accurate observations and measurements

This skill is one which very clearly distinguishes one student from another.

Making observations

It is important when making observations to make *all* of the possible observations and not just some of them. What should you be looking for? All changes have some significance although you might not realize exactly what, until later. It is rather like Sherlock Holmes looking for clues. It is often the tiniest detail, which Dr Watson – and some of us – would not notice, which enables Sherlock Holmes to solve the case. He can then say, 'Elementary, my dear Watson'.

In an experiment involving chemical change you might look for:
- change of colour
- change of state e.g. solid → liquid
- gas evolved
- formation of precipitate
- temperature changes showing either an exothermic or an endothermic reaction
- crackling noises when a substance is heated.

The heating of a sample of sulphur in a test tube might lead to the following observations:
- sulphur melts at low temperature
- it forms a pale amber coloured liquid
- the liquid is free-flowing (mobile) at this stage
- on further heating the liquid goes darker eventually turning black
- at this stage liquid is treacle-like (viscous)
- liquid sulphur boils
- sulphur catches alight
- it burns with a blue flame
- it gives off a gas with a choking smell

Better students will make most of these observations but weaker candidates will only make a few.

Example

Here is an opportunity for you to test your powers of observation.

Figure 4.3 shows four different species of wood louse. Look at these carefully and then describe one way that each of them is different from the other three. Ignore any differences in size.

Look at *Oniscus* first. It has only six pairs of legs visible. All of the others have seven pairs. *Porcellio* is spotted and the others are not. *Armadillidium* has no *cerci* (pair of 'tails'). *Philoscia* has a different arrangement of rear legs.

There are examples in Section Five in which you can make observations. The following checklist summarizes some things you should remember when making observations.

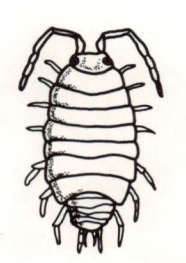

Philoscia muscorum   Armadillidium vulgare   Porcellio scaber   Oniscus asellus (Antenna, Head, Segment, Leg, Cercus)

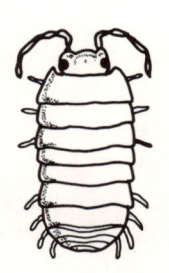

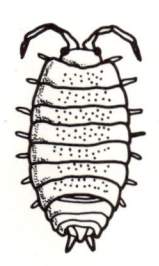

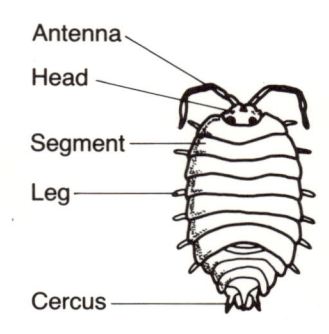

Fig. 4.3 Four different types of wood louse

✓ Checklist 4.1 Observations

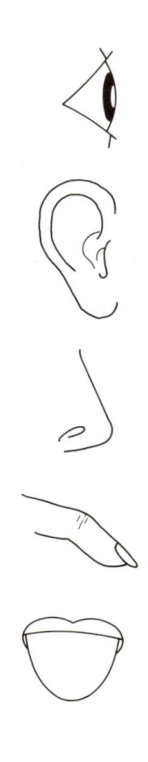

When carrying out experiments you must use all of your senses.

Sight: Most of your observations will be seen. Sometimes you will be asked to make observations of changes during an experiment. At other times you will be asked to compare with a **standard**, e.g. a pH chart, or to compare two specimens. Try to make your observations detailed, e.g. 'canary yellow', 'mustard yellow', 'pale yellow' are better than just 'yellow'.

NB If you are colour-blind ensure that your teacher knows.

Sound: You may be required to listen to sounds or you may hear sounds during experiments. Try to judge both volume and frequency of sounds.

Smell: You may be expected to observe certain smells during experiments. Smell any gas produced *cautiously*. Try to recognize familiar smells.

Touch: You should only touch apparatus, chemicals or biological specimens when you are *told* to do so. **Never** touch electrical apparatus with wet hands. Look for familiar textures, e.g. rough, smooth, soapy. You may also feel slight temperature changes.

Taste: Never taste anything in a science lesson unless you are *told* to do so. If you are told to taste something, try to recognize familiar tastes, e.g. salty, sweet, sour, spicy, bitter.

Making measurements

You will make a large number of measurements during practical lessons and assessments. Figure 4.4 shows a number of scales and dials. They are all relatively easy measurements for you to make. Check your answers with those on page 21.

(a) Rule

(b) Measuring cylinder

(c) Burette

(d) Thermometer

(e)

❛Do not overlook obvious changes when making observations.❜

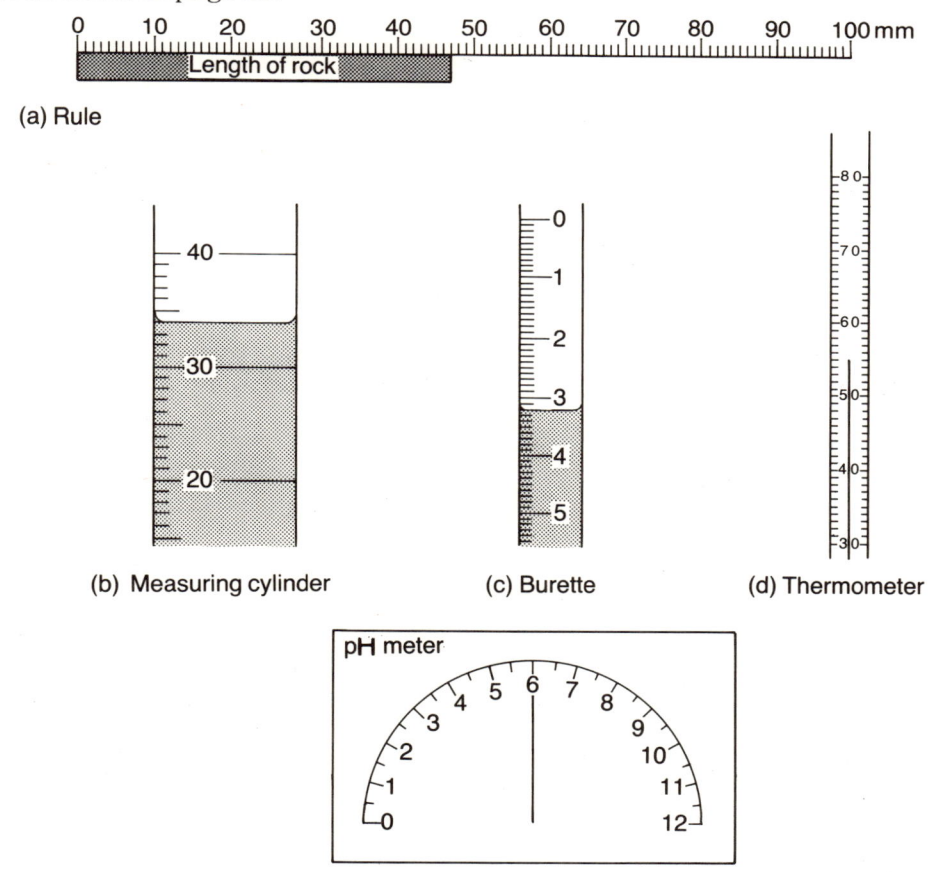

Fig. 4.4 Scales and dials which are easy to read. (Don't forget the units!)

(a) Rule

When taking measurements during an experiment take more than you need. You can always discard results you do not require.

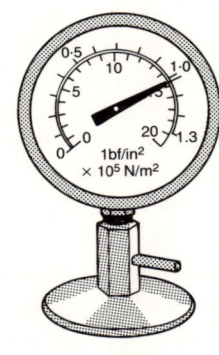

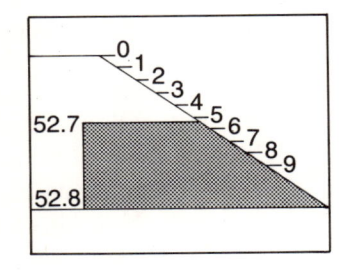

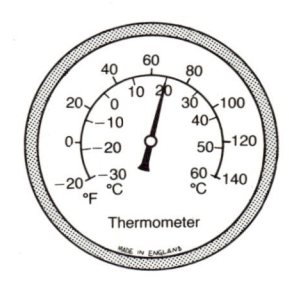

(b) Pressure gauge

(c) Top pan balance

(d) Dial thermometer

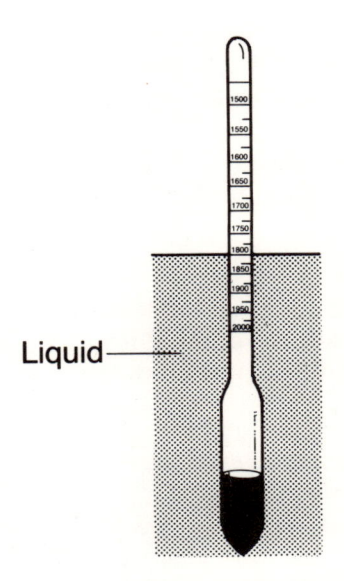

(e) Hydrometer

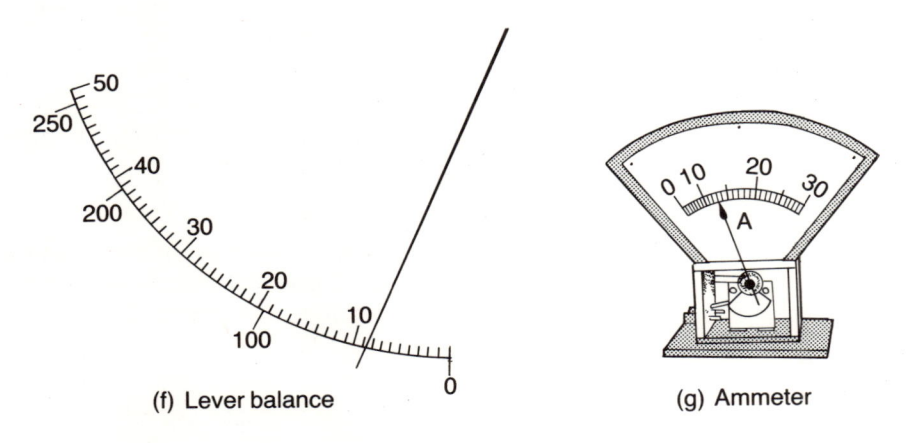

(f) Lever balance

(g) Ammeter

Fig. 4.5 Scales and dials which are more difficult to read

Figure 4.5 contains some more difficult examples where you have to exercise a little more judgment. You may find some of these harder to do.

When reading any kind of measuring instrument it is important to have your eye in the correct place. Figure 4.6 shows a measuring cylinder being read correctly, with the eye level with the water level. This is to avoid error. Voltmeters and ammeters often include small mirrors under the scale. You make sure that the real needle covers the image of the needle in the mirror, and so avoid error.

Reading a scale to the required accuracy is an important part of a GCSE science assessment.

(d) Recording your results accurately

It is worth remembering that it is only the results you record that can be marked or assessed. You may have *made* the best observations or measurements but unless you *record* them you cannot be given credit.

An orderly method of recording information is something an assessor looks for. Often your teacher will give you a table in which to record your results. There may, however, be times when you have to design your own table for results. This is particularly so when your teacher is trying to devise experiments for you to demonstrate your proficiency in this skill at the highest level.

Fig. 4.6 A measuring cylinder being used correctly

Example

Suppose you are carrying out an experiment to measure how the extension of a spring changes when different masses are hung from it.

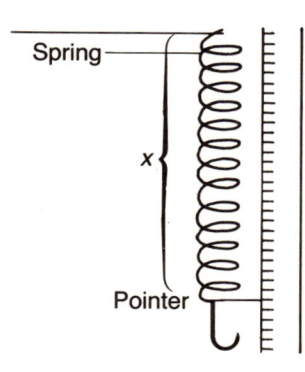

Fig. 4.7 Setting up the experiment

You start with the apparatus set up as in Figure 4.7. The length of the spring with no mass on the end is 10.0 cm. The first mass you try is 200 g and the length of the spring (x in the diagram) is 11.7 cm. Then you put a 100 g mass on and the length is 10.8 cm. Then you put both the 100 g and 200 g masses on and the length x is 12.4 cm. Then you put an extra 200 g on (making 500 g) and $x = 14.0$ cm. Finally you take the 100 g mass off and $x = 13.1$ cm.

(This may seem a very haphazard way of doing it but an assessor sees many haphazard attempts at practical work! You should *try* to be logical in what you do.)

The results can be recorded in a table like the one below.

Mass on spring (in g)	Original length (in cm)	Length of spring (in cm)	Extension (in cm)
100	10.0	10.8	0.8
200	10.0	11.7	1.7
300	10.0	12.4	2.4
400	10.0	13.1	3.1
500	10.0	14.0	4.0

It helps you later on if you get your results into some kind of order. In this case we have used increasing mass on the spring as the starting point. It is usual to arrange the results in *ascending* or *increasing* order. It is better to take more measurements than you think you will require. This means that you can ignore any obviously wrong ones. Your results can be plotted on a graph.

There are different types of graph. One type of graph is a **bar graph** which you will have drawn before. Figure 4.8 is a bar graph showing the increases in mass that different students found when they heated a metal in a Bunsen burner flame.

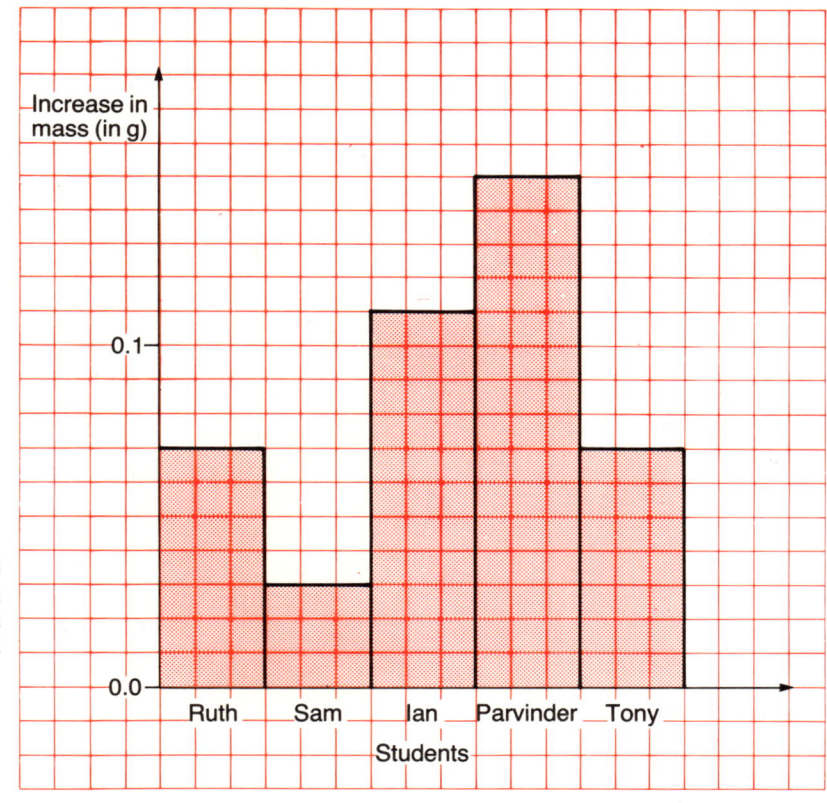

❛*When recording results involving decimals, keep the decimal points under one another.*
e.g. 38.2   not 38.2
     4.17   4.17❜

Fig. 4.8 Increases in mass when heating metal

From this bar graph, you can conclude that Parvinder obtained the largest increase in mass and Sam the smallest. There is no pattern in these results. They are just five isolated experiments and a bar graph is a good way of showing them.

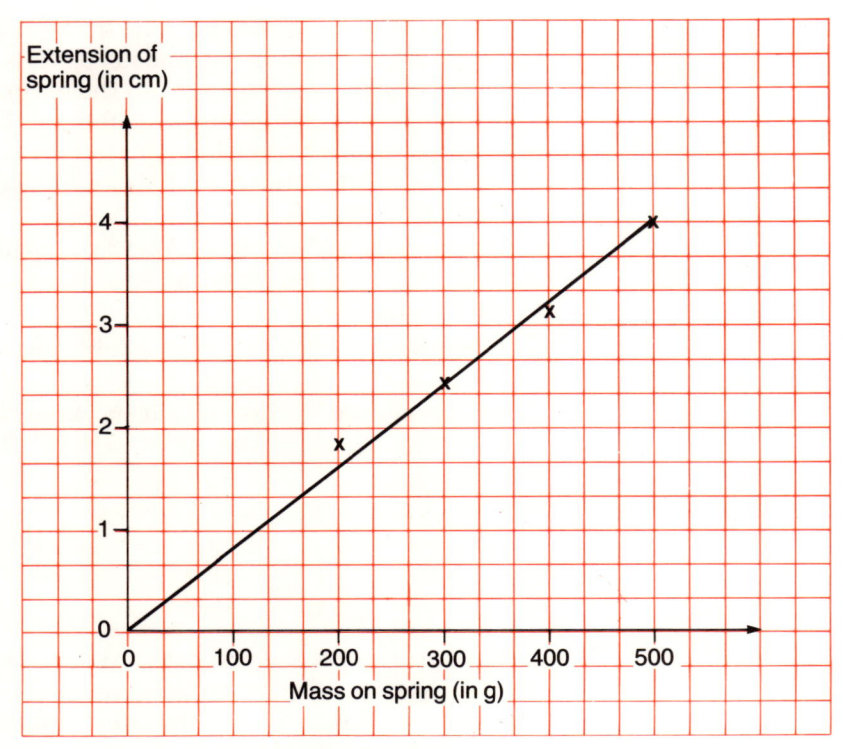

Fig. 4.9 The extension of a spring

In sciences we use graphs like the one in Figure 4.9 very widely. Your teacher might give you a piece of paper with the axes already drawn, which makes the task easier. You may, on the other hand, be given a blank piece of graph paper. If this is so, remember:

1 Use a sharp pencil to draw the graphs.

2 Draw the axes first. Label the axes, e.g. 'Extension in cm' and 'Mass on spring in g'. Choose a good scale on each axis so that the graph covers at least half of the piece of graph paper. The scales are then written in ascending order.

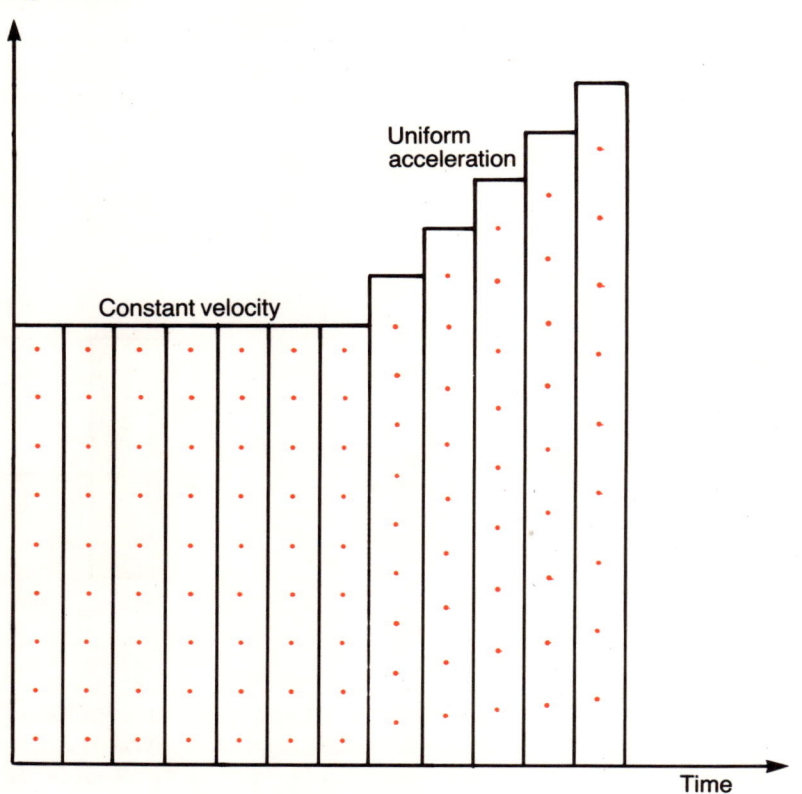

> **❛**When plotting graphs, ensure you always label the axes and give a clear scale on each axis.**❜**

Fig. 4.10 A bar chart from tickertape

3 Plot the points carefully, either with a small cross (x) or ⊙. The assessor will accept either.

4 Draw the graph with a good straight line or a good curve. Do not draw the line too thick. Your line will not necessarily pass through all points. It should be the best line you can draw. This is called 'the line of best fit' by scientists.

You will notice in the case of our extending spring that the points do not all fall on a perfect straight line. In science we have **experimental errors**. We can make slight errors, for example, in measuring the length of the spring. The points on the graph are not all perfect. This makes science different from mathematics. If you plot a graph of $y = 2x + 1$ for values of x between -5 and $+5$ you get a straight line.

There are other ways of recording results. **Block graphs** are not used widely in sciences, but in experiments with tickertape timers on speed and acceleration, good block graphs can be plotted using the strips of tickertape produced in the experiment.

Results can also be displayed in **diagrams** and **charts**. When drawing diagrams try and keep everything simple. Leave out anything which is not important and which would take the eye away from the main point. Draw diagrams in pencil, making sure that you do not draw them too small. You can use a ruler, if you have time. Otherwise, try to draw neat freehand diagrams. Label the diagrams in ink. Give each diagram a clear heading. In biology you may have to record your observations by drawing freehand sketches. You will see examples in Sections Five and Six.

(e) Drawing conclusions from results

Having got a set of results you might then be expected to make conclusions *from* these results. Sometimes, if you have a poor set of results, it may be impossible to draw any conclusions. Your conclusions **must** fit the results that you have.

In the experiment with the spring it is reasonable for you to conclude that increasing the mass on the spring increases the length of the spring regularly. You might also conclude that an extra 100 g mass will extend the spring by a further 0.8 cm. The extension of the spring is **proportional** to the mass on the spring.

If you arrange the results in a logical order, drawing conclusions becomes easier.

Example

In a chemical reaction between sodium thiosulphate solution and dilute hydrochloric acid, the time is measured until the solution goes cloudy due to the formation of insoluble sulphur and a cross disappears when viewed

> ❝*When drawing conclusions from results, look for results which do not 'fit in'. Do not let one or two odd results put you off. Repeat them if it is possible. Try to explain why these results are out.*❞

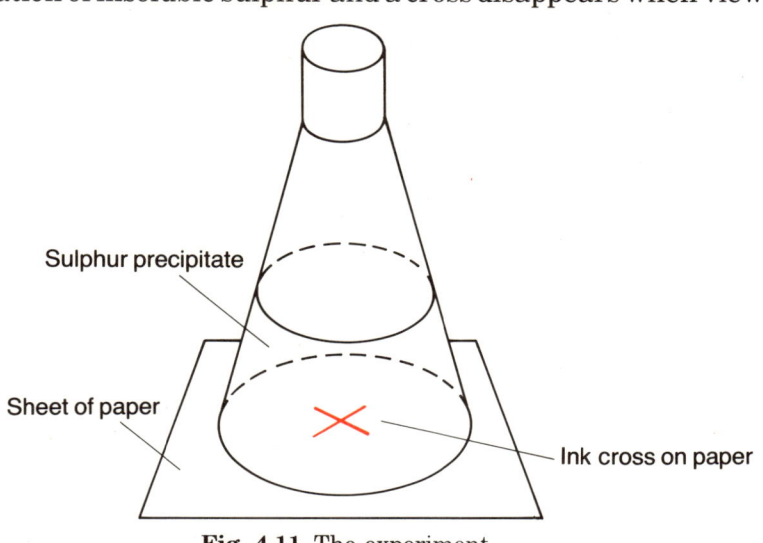

Fig. 4.11 The experiment

through the solution (Figure 4.11). The results were recorded in the table below by a student (Figure 4.12).

Volume of solution in cm³ at the top of the column would avoid units having to be put in each time.

Experiments not in a logical order which will make conclusions easier to draw. Order could be (II), (IV), (V), (I), (VI), or (VI), (I), (V), (IV), (II).

	Volume of sodium thiosulphate (cm³)	Volume of hydrochloric acid (cm³)	Volume of water (cm³)	Total Volume	Time taken for cross to disappear
(I)	35	5	15	55	25 sec
(II)	5	5	45	55	1.50 min
(III)	25	5	25	55 cm³	35 sec
(IV)	10	5	40	55	1 min 15 sec
(V)	15	5	30	50 cm³	1 min
(VI)	45	5	5	55	20 sec

Solution has a different volume to other experiments.

Serious mistake! Times recorded incorrectly due to confusion with minutes and seconds. — 1 min 50 secs wrongly recorded as 1.50 minutes

Fig. 4.12 A student's results

Let us look briefly at this table before drawing conclusions.
- All of the experiments except (v) have a total volume of 55 cm³ so that the student is viewing through the same volume of solution each time.
- The time is recorded incorrectly. 1.50 minutes means one and a half minutes i.e. 90 seconds. The student has written 1 minute 50 seconds incorrectly. This is a very frequent mistake. It is advisable to use *either* seconds *or* minutes throughout.

Let us draw a conclusion from this experiment. What changes do we see in these experiments?
The two important ones are:
- the volume of sodium thiosulphate *increases*
- the time for the reaction *decreases*.

We can therefore write the conclusion:
The time for the reaction decreases as the volume of sodium thiosulphate increases.
We can refine this if we remember:
1 A reaction which takes a long time is a slow reaction and a reaction which is completed quickly is a fast reaction.
2 A solution which has a larger volume of sodium thiosulphate in 55 cm³ of solution is more concentrated.
We can, therefore, write,
The rate of reaction increases as the concentration of the reactant increases.
This is the most correct conclusion that you could draw.

(f) Testing hypotheses, planning simple experiments and problem-solving

This is a very important aspect of GCSE in sciences. The planning of *whole experiments* is something that researchers have found students have difficulty doing. The practical assessments for GCSE have shown that this skill is least well developed in all students.

What is an hypothesis? The dictionary defines hypothesis (plural-*hypotheses*) as 'a supposition made as a basis for reasoning, without assumption of its truth'. It is, then, the starting point, with further investigation, for establishing a theory. A theory is far more certain. As a result of your experiments, or somebody else's, it may be possible to produce a simple hypothesis to explain the experimental results. You may then be asked to plan further investigations to confirm the truth of the hypothesis.

Example

Objects are dropped out of a window and fall ten metres to the ground. The results are shown below.

Fall quickly to the ground: steel ball, aluminium ball
Fall slowly to the ground: piece of paper, piece of polystyrene sheet

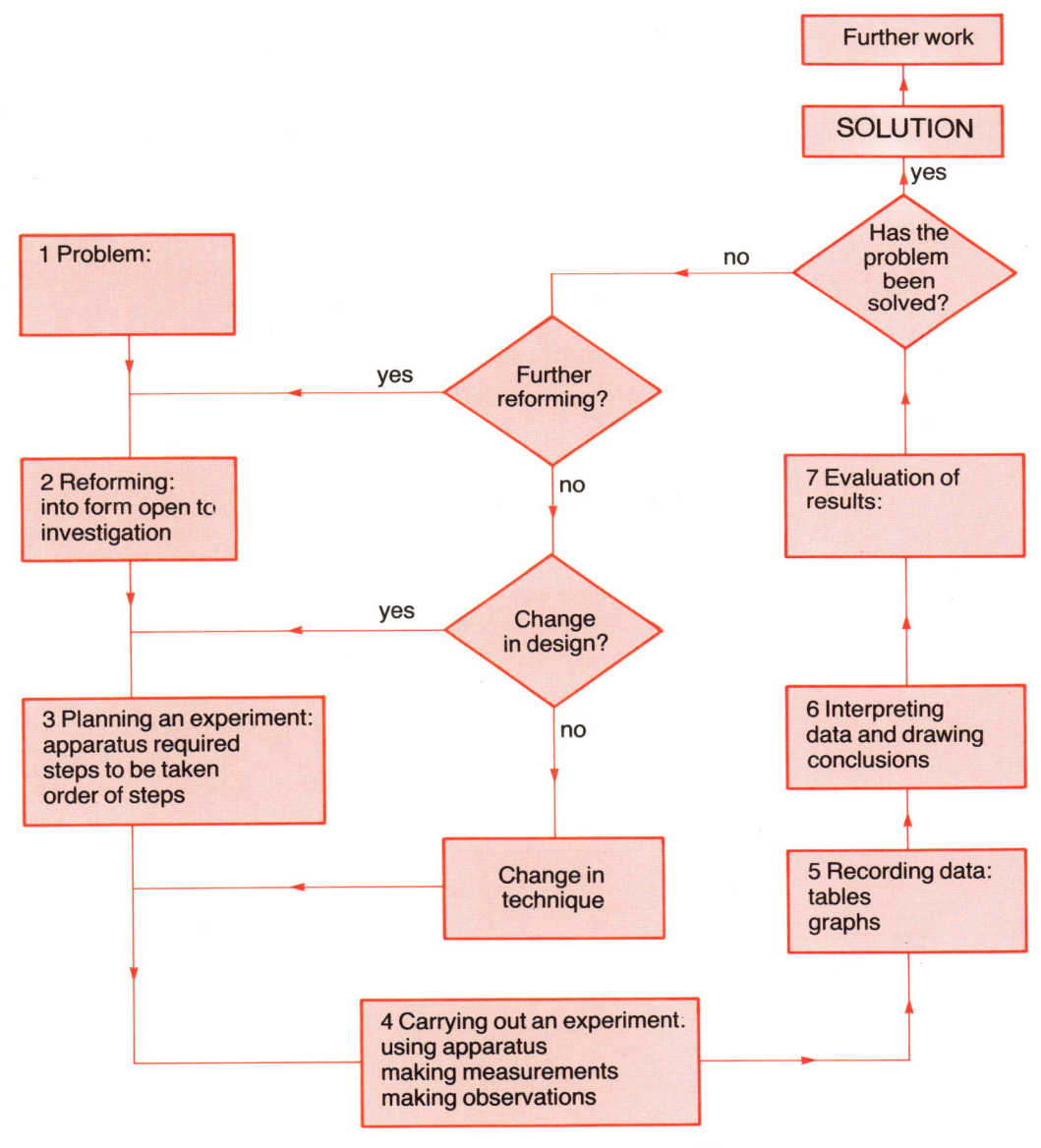

Fig. 4.13 Steps in solving a problem

A simple hypothesis based upon this evidence could be that heavy objects fall quickly and light objects fall slowly. This is a reasonable hypothesis on the basis of the evidence available.

In order to test this hypothesis, experiments could be carried out using balls of screwed up paper, polystyrene, steel and aluminium, all of the same size. Each ball is weighed and the four balls are dropped at the same time from the window. When you find all four balls land *together* you have to go back and revise the original hypothesis! A new hypothesis could then be devised which could be tested again.

It is important to remember that in any exercise to test an hypothesis or to plan an experiment to solve a problem, there is *never* one right answer. There will be a variety of possible solutions of varying merit and they will be marked accordingly.

It is important to understand the processes through which we must go to solve a problem. These are summarized in Fig. 4.13.

Having been given the problem to be solved (number 1 on the diagram), the first stage is to get the problem into a form that you can investigate (number 2 on the diagram). You will probably have met something similar. Think of any similar experiments you have tried or seen. Do not try to find difficult solutions to the problem at this stage. Your approach can be further sophisticated at a later stage.

Having decided on your approach it is necessary to plan an experiment carefully (number 3). List all the apparatus etc. that you will require and the steps which have to be taken, in the correct order. Finally, check your experiment through and make up your own mind about whether it will work. Often at this stage you will realize that there is something you have missed out. Students, for example, frequently forget to include a stopclock in an experiment where a series of timings have to be made.

Carry out the experiment carefully according to your plan (number 4).

During the experiment you will have made a number of observations and measurements. Record these as well as you can using tables where possible. You may be able to plot your results onto a graph. This is number 5.

> *When planning an experiment with a control, check that only one variable is changed at a time.*

Next, look at your results, without any preconceived ideas, and try to interpret the results and come up with conclusions (number 6).

Then you must look carefully at what you have concluded and go back to the original problem. Does your answer actually solve the problem you were set? Think carefully and do not rush this stage (number 7). The chances are that your experiment was not as good as it could have been. We can always think of improvements afterwards. Now is the time to incorporate these. You might consider that you could improve:

- the whole basis of the investigation (number 2)
- the planning of the experiment (number 3)
- the carrying out of the experiment (number 4).

After repeating the process – perhaps a number of times – you should reach a solution to the problem. This process sounds rather long and unwieldy but perhaps can be seen better in an actual problem.

Problem

You are given a metal rod about 1 m long. Devise an experiment to show that it expands when it is heated.

Your first thought might be to try and measure it exactly when it is cold and again when it is hot. However, you will perhaps realize that the expansion is small and probably not measurable. There would probably be a problem measuring a hot rod anyway. You might initially *try* this, but when the results are unsatisfactory you would go back and reformulate the problem.

Perhaps the solution can be found in magnifying the expansion? If one end is fixed and the rod is free to move over rollers, it may be possible to

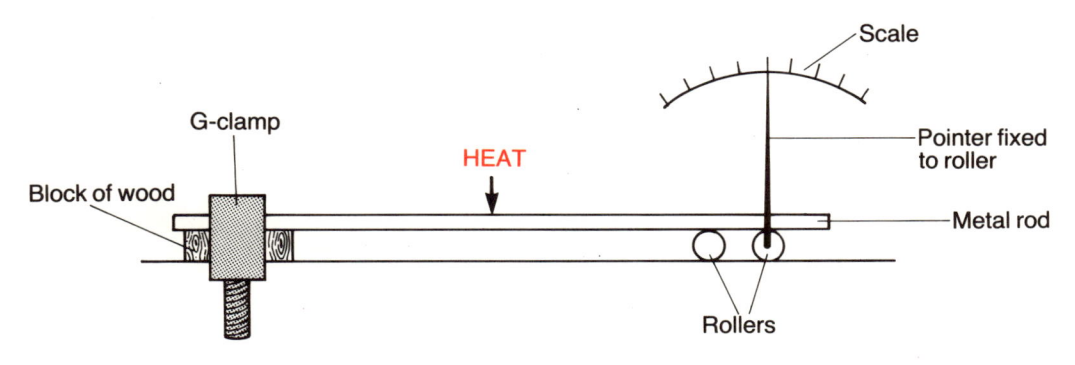

Fig. 4.14 Will this work?

fix a pointer to one of the rollers. The apparatus set up in Figure 4.14 might therefore be suitable.

Having carried out this experiment and considered the results, you might be able to think of further improvements in the experiment.

Problem

Do seeds grow faster in the presence of some mineral salt solutions than others?

You would obviously choose something like mustard seed which germinates well. Prepare a number of Petri dishes, each containing blotting paper soaked in a different salt solution. You sprinkle equal numbers of mustard seeds onto the blotting paper in each Petri dish. The seeds are allowed to germinate and grow under the same conditions. At the end of the experiment you have to devise some way of comparing the growth of the seeds in the different Petri dishes.

One idea you might have is to weigh each Petri dish and contents at the start and finish of the experiment. The increase in mass would be the mass of mustard plants produced. However, you would have forgotten one factor. The water in the salt solution would have evaporated. Could you be sure that the evaporation in each case would be the same? You probably could not and so you would abandon that approach.

An alternative would be to harvest the plants in each case and put each set of plants on a separate, previously weighed watch glass. The watch glasses and plants could be dried in an oven at 100 °C for the same length of time and then reweighed. This seems a fair comparison.

Summary of problem solving

1 What is it that the problem is asking you to do?
2 Is there anything that can be easily measured?
3 Are there already apparatus/instruments available to help with measuring?
4 Think of as many ways of tackling the problem as possible.
5 Finally choose which appears to be the best.

(g) Suggesting improvements to experiments

This is really an extension of (**f**). If you have carried out an investigation practically you should have looked for improvements as you went along. Few experiments are so perfect that they cannot be improved. Often a teacher, because he or she does an experiment many times, fails to see ways in which the experiment could be improved. A fresh mind is often better at suggesting improvements.

Example

Let us consider a simple experiment. You are asked to burn a piece of magnesium ribbon and find the mass of magnesium oxide formed. The experiment could be carried out in a crucible and lid (Figure 4.15).

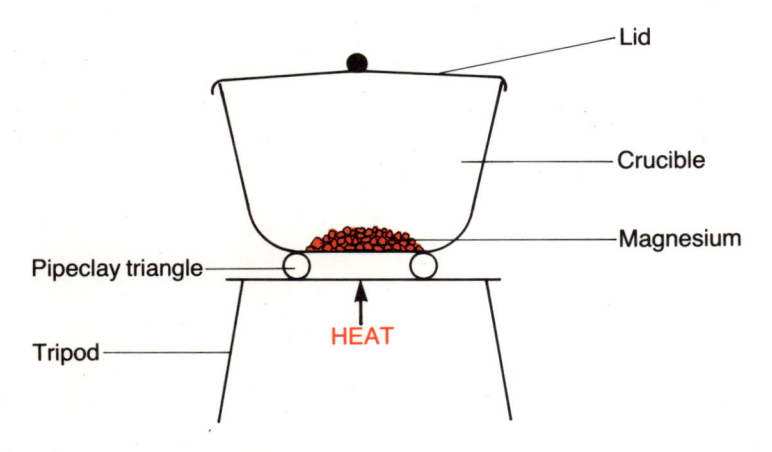

Fig. 4.15 Burning magnesium ribbon

However, the lid would have to be lifted from time to time to allow air to enter the crucible as oxygen is required for burning. If you are told that magnesium also burns in nitrogen, you might realize that there are imperfections in the experiment.

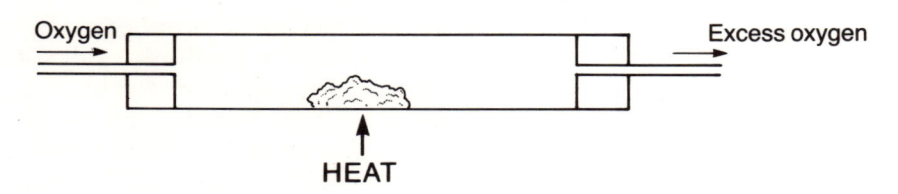

Fig. 4.16 A suggestion

Figure 4.16 shows one suggestion from a student as to how the experiment could be carried out. Pure oxygen is passed over heated magnesium. This would avoid the problem of magnesium reacting with nitrogen but would be dangerous because the magnesium would burn too well. What improvement could you suggest to this experiment?

One idea would be to mix together oxygen and, perhaps, argon. Argon is a **noble gas** and does not react with magnesium. It would slow down the reaction of magnesium with oxygen.

You will now find in Section Five a whole series of questions based upon practical situations. If you work carefully through these you should find your practical skills will improve.

✓ **Checklist 4.2: Improving an experiment**

1 Look at the aim of the experiment.

2 Look at the method suggested.

3 List any faults or deficiencies with the method suggested:
(a) look at the apparatus used
(b) look at the steps to be taken
(c) look at the order of the steps.

4 Suggest improvements to the experiments under the same three headings as in **3**.

5 Go back to the aim of the experiment and check that the suggestions you have made improve the experiment and do not invalidate it.

Answers to questions

Safety in the laboratory (page 9)

Likely causes of an accident:
- fire exit doors obstructed by a box
- concentrated acid stored on a narrow, high shelf
- cupboard door left open
- bottle of 'pop' in the laboratory
- water tap left on
- tripod very near the edge of the bench
- person picking up a bottle by its neck
- broken apparatus on the bench
- wet patch on the floor
- fire extinguisher is missing
- poison cupboard left open
- a thermometer is near the edge of the bench
- curtains hanging near the Bunsen burner
- a stool is left blocking a gangway
- Petri dish lid removed from culture of bacteria
- electrical apparatus in close proximity to pool of water
- microscope near the edge of bench

Measurements (pages 11-12)

Fig. 4.4: **(a)** 47 mm; **(b)** 34 cm^3; **(c)** 3.2 cm^3; **(d)** 55 °C; **(e)** pH 6

Fig. 4.5: **(a)** 62 mm; **(b)** 15 lbf/in^2 (or 1×10^5 N/m^2); **(c)** 52.75 g; **(d)** 20 °C (70 °F); **(e)** 1.800; **(f)** 48 g; **(g)** 13 A

SECTION FIVE

Questions to develop practical skills

Summary of skills tested by questions in Section Five

Skills tested:
- **(a)** following instructions
- **(b)** selecting and using apparatus safely
- **(c)** making accurate observations and measurements
- **(d)** recording accurately
- **(e)** drawing conclusions from results
- **(f)** planning simple experiments, testing hypotheses and problem solving
- **(g)** suggesting improvements to experiments

Subjects:
- S   science
- P   physics
- C   chemistry
- B   biology

Question number	S	P	C	B	(a)	(b)	(c)	(d)	(e)	(f)	(g)
1	•			•	•		•			•	
2	•			•			•			•	
3	•	•						•	•		
4	•							•	•	•	
5	•		•						•		
6	•									•	
7	•		•			•				•	
8	•		•			•					
9			•								•
10	•			•			•				
11	•						•	•			•
12	•		•				•		•		
13	•							•	•		
14	•						•		•		
15	•			•			•			•	
16	•			•			•				
17	•		•			•				•	•
18	•		•			•				•	
19			•			•					
20		•	•				•				
21	•			•			•				
22	•	•									
23	•	•								•	
24	•						•	•	•	•	

Question number	S	P	C	B	(a)	(b)	(c)	(d)	(e)	(f)	(g)
25	•									•	
26	•		•		•					•	
27			•							•	
28	•						•	•	•		
29	•						•	•	•	•	
30			•							•	
31	•									•	
32	•						•			•	
33	•	•									•
34	•	•					•			•	
35				•						•	
36	•		•							•	
37	•									•	•
38	•		•			•	•	•		•	•
39	•		•				•	•		•	
40	•									•	
41	•	•	•			•	•	•	•	•	•
42	•	•				•	•	•	•	•	•
43	•	•					•	•	•	•	
44	•		•				•		•	•	
45	•			•						•	

1 Below is a key which can be used to identify some of the gulls commonly found in Great Britain.

(1)	Head black or dark brown	Go to (2)
	Head white	Go to (3)
(2)	Black markings on upper surface of wings	Black-headed gull
	No black markings on upper surface of wings	Little gull
(3)	Back black or dark	Go to (4)
	Back grey or pale	Go to (5)
(4)	Legs flesh coloured	Great black-backed gull
	Legs yellow or orange	Lesser black-backed gull
(5)	Wing tips solid black	Kittiwake
	Wing tips black with white patches	Go to (6)
(6)	Thick yellow bill with red spot	Herring gull
	Thin greenish bill without red spot	Common gull

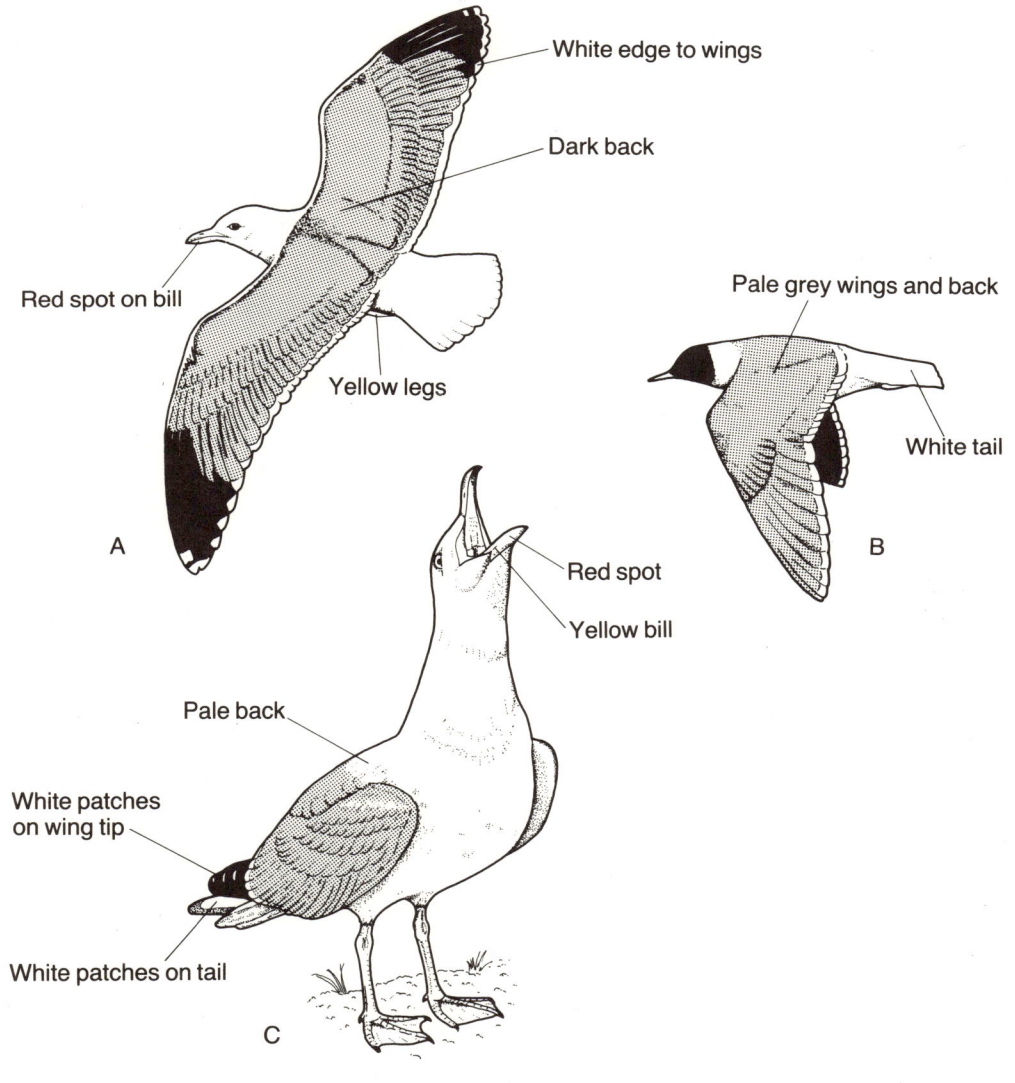

Fig. 5.1 Gulls

(a) The drawings in Figure 5.1 are sketches made by a bird-watcher while observing some gulls. Use the key above to identify the gulls A, B and C.

Skills (a) and (c)

(b) The birdwatcher also caught glimpse of a gull with a white head, solid black wing tips and a pale grey back. Which type of gull was this? *Skill (a)*

(c) Explain why you could not be certain of the identification of a gull if you only had time to see a white head and black and white wing tips.
Skill (a)

(d) Some types of gull have red spots on their bills. When a parent gull brings food to the young in the nest, the young birds peck at the red spot. The parent opens its bill to allow the young birds to get the food held in it.

It is suggested that the young gulls are stimulated to peck at the bill by the red spot. It is also possible that the young gulls are stimulated to peck by the shape of the bill.

How would you test whether either of these suggestions is true? *Skills (f)*

◇S◇ ◇B◇ **2** Figure 5.2 shows the larval stages, called 'nymphs', of two insects, the stonefly and the mayfly. The nymphs live in streams. They have flattened bodies and crawl around on stones at the bottom of the stream, often staying underneath the stones in fast-flowing rivers.

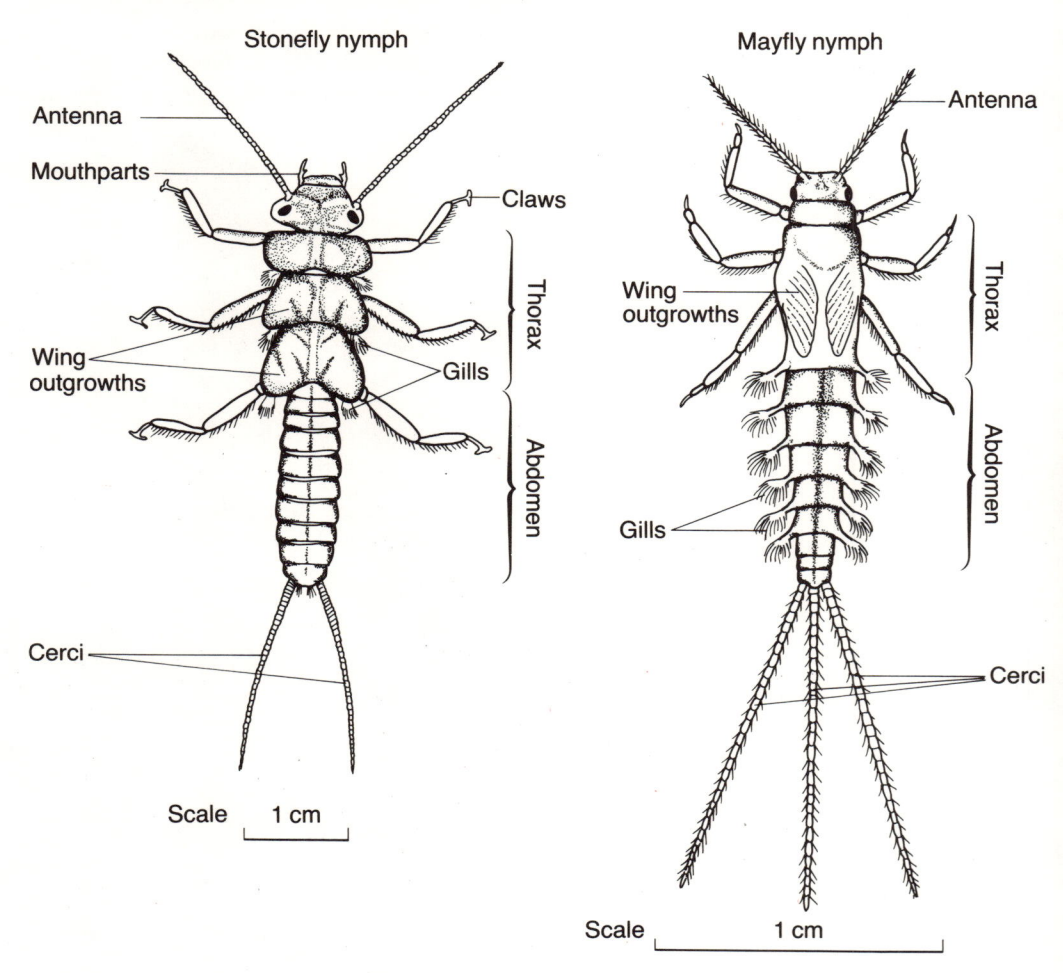

Fig. 5.2 Nymphs

(a) Complete the table, listing ten differences between the stonefly and the mayfly.

Stoneyfly nymph	**Mayfly nymph**
(1) Hairless antennae (2)	Hairy antennae

Skills (c) and (d)

(b) Use the scales to calculate the length of the body of each nymph (from the tip of the head to the tip of the abdomen). *Skill (d)*

(c) Give two ways in which the nymphs are adapted for living in fast-flowing rivers. *Skill (f)*

3 You are asked to find if the resistance of a small electrical heater changes when the current in it is increased. You are given the apparatus in Figure 5.3.

Fig. 5.3 The apparatus

(a) Draw a circuit diagram to show how you would connect them together. *Skill (f)*

(b) Some sample results are shown in the table below.

Potential difference (in V)	Current (in A)	Resistance (in Ω)
1.0	0.5	
2.3	1.1	
3.5	1.6	
4.8	2.2	
6.2	2.7	
7.1	3.2	
7.9	3.7	
9.2	4.2	

Use a grid like the one in Figure 5.4 to plot a graph of potential difference against current. *Skill (d)*

Fig. 5.4 The graph

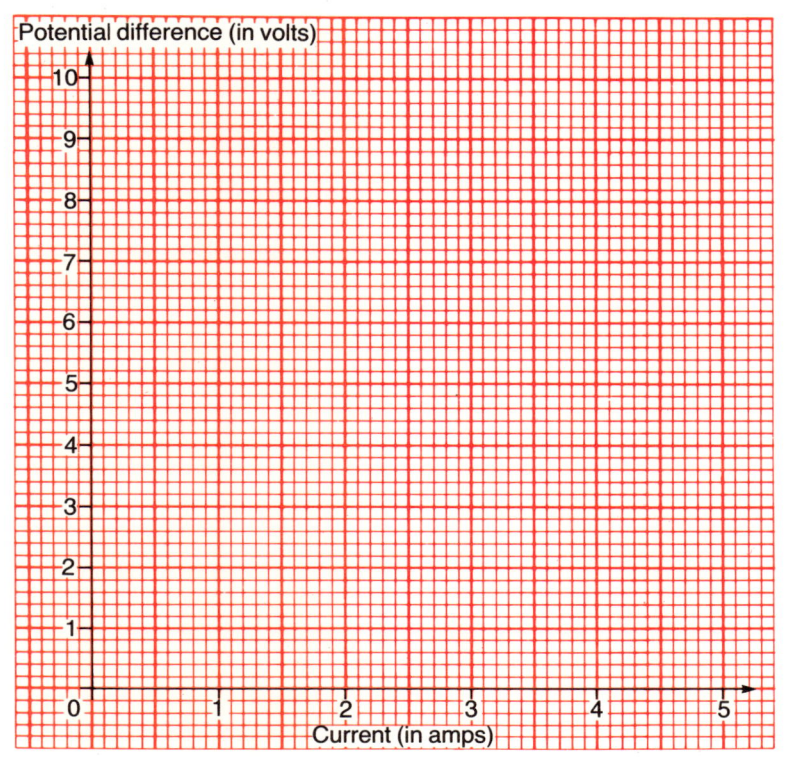

(c) Complete the last column of the table by calculating the resistance for each set of readings. Here is an example to show you how to do this, using the last pair of values in the table.

First the formula:
    resistance = potential difference ÷ current
Now substitute the numbers:
    resistance = 9.2 V ÷ 4.2 A
Finally, the answer and unit:
    = 2.2 Ω   *Skill (d)*

(d) What can you conclude about the resistance of the heater? As the current gets bigger, does the resistance get bigger, get smaller or stay the same? What feature of the graph indicates that this is the case?   *Skill (e)*

4 This question is about an experiment which involved the use of a thermistor to measure temperature. Sunil set up the circuit shown in Figure 5.5.

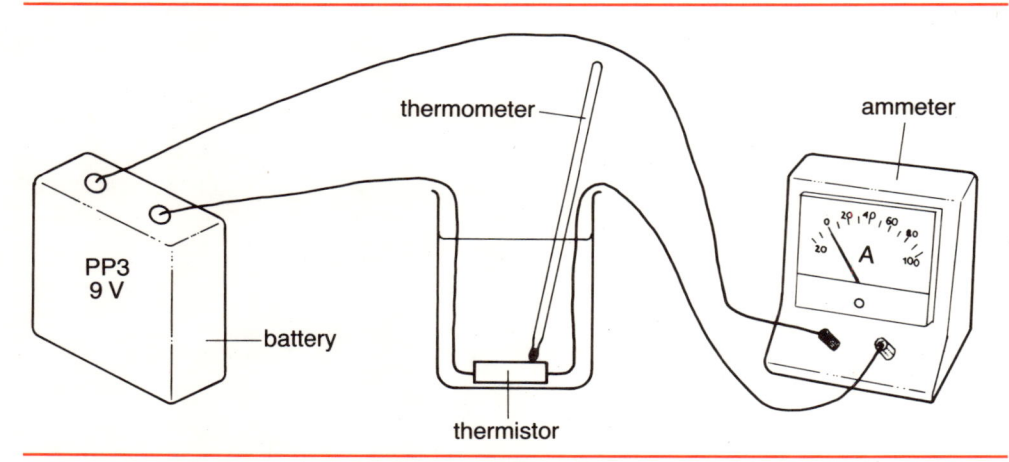

Fig. 5.5 The circuit

He put the thermistor into a beaker of water, with the thermometer. He took readings of the current in the thermistor at different temperatures, and used the value of 9.0 V to calculate the resistance at these temperatures. He used this equation.

resistance = potential difference ÷ current

The diagrams in Figure 5.6 show the ammeter and thermometer readings as they were when he took the results.

(a) Write down the thermometer and ammeter results in a suitable table.   *Skills (c) and (d)*

(b) Work out the resistance at each temperature and put your results in the form of a table, with 'Resistance' in one column and 'Temperature' in the other.   *Skill (d)*

(c) Use a grid like the one in Figure 5.7 on page 28 to plot a graph of resistance (up, i.e. on the *y*-axis) against temperature (across, i.e. on the *x*-axis).   *Skill (d)*

(d) Write a short conclusion about the way in which the resistance changes.   *Skill (e)*

(e) Elaine then measures the resistance of the thermistor to be 45 Ω when she puts it into a locust cage. Use your graph to estimate the temperature of the locust cage.   *Skill (f)*

5 Joe Bloggs was arrested by the police for breaking into a gardening shop. He was found to have two white substances, labelled A and B, on his clothes. He claimed that these were flour and caster sugar, because his wife had been using them to make cakes and he had got in the way! The police had found that two bags of chemicals had been damaged in the

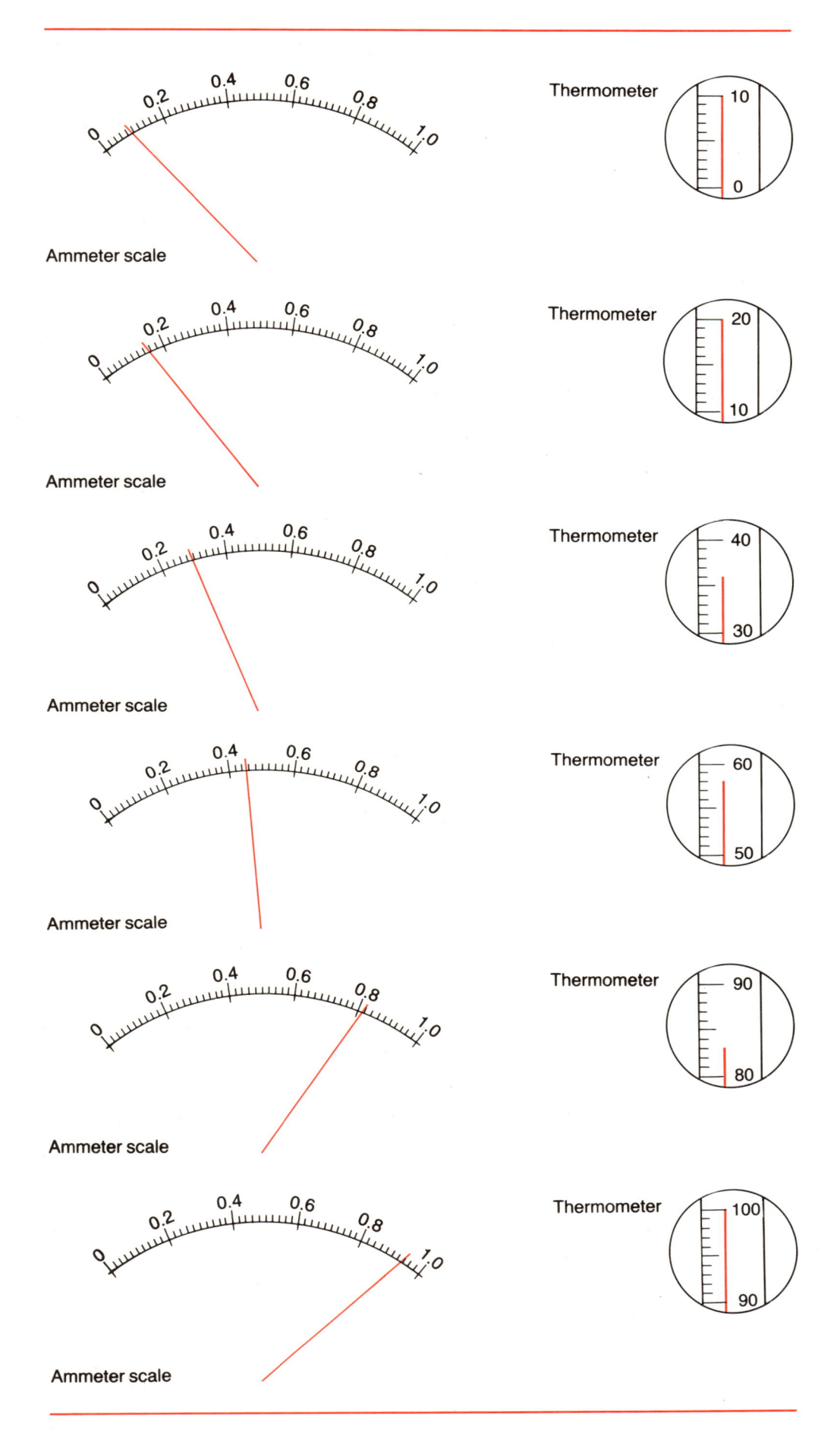

Fig. 5.6 The readings

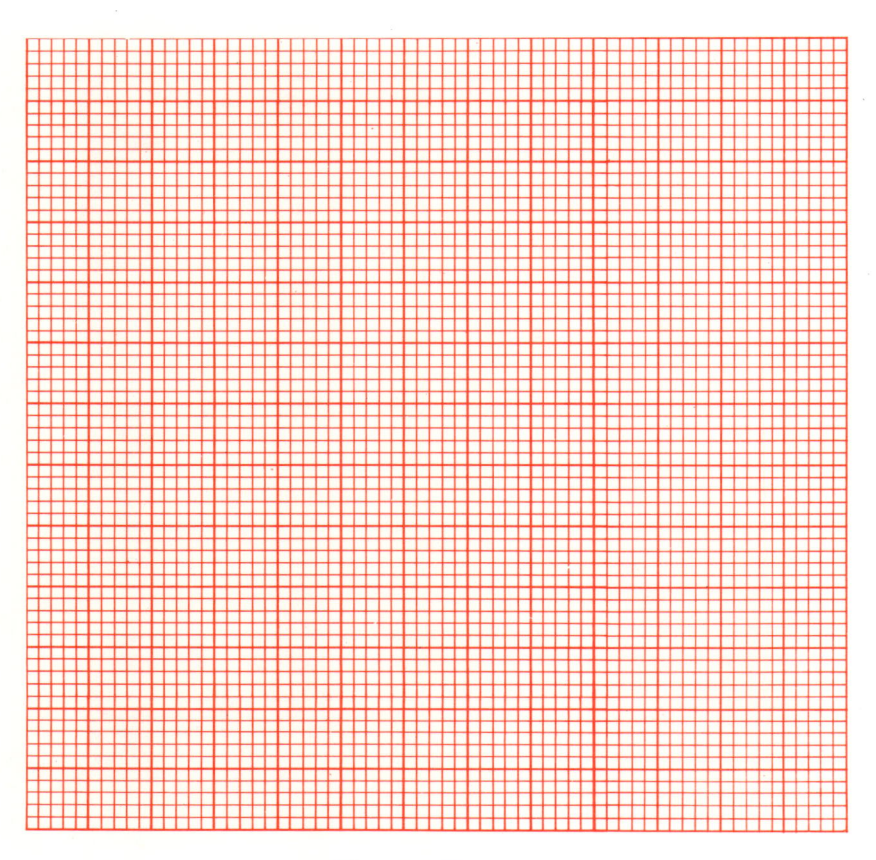

Fig. 5.7 The Grid

gardening shop during the break-in. One was a fertilizer made from sulphate of ammonia and the other was garden lime. The forensic scientist carried out a simple experiment on A and B and also on the four possible substances flour, caster sugar, sulphate of ammonia and garden lime. The results are shown in the table below.

Substance	Test with Universal indicator	Test with litmus
A	golden yellow	pink
B	purple	blue
flour	green	pink
caster sugar	green	purple
sulphate of ammonia	golden yellow	pink
garden lime	purple	blue

(a) Using the table, what substances do you think that A and B are? *Skill (e)*
(b) On the basis of this evidence, do you think that Joe Bloggs is guilty?
Skill (e)

⟨S⟩ ⟨C⟩ 6 Read carefully the following information about carbon monoxide.
Carbon monoxide:

> *(1)* Is very poisonous.
> *(2)* Has a density very similar to that of the air.
> *(3)* Does not dissolve in water.
> *(4)* Can be prepared by passing carbon dioxide gas over hot lumps of charcoal. Not all of the carbon dioxide is converted to carbon monoxide, however.
> *(5)* Unlike carbon dioxide, does not dissolve in potassium hydroxide solution.

Assuming that you have a gas cylinder of carbon dioxide and all of the usual laboratory apparatus, draw and label a diagram to show how you would make and collect several gas jars filled with carbon monoxide.

Skill (f)

⟨S⟩ ⟨B⟩ ⟨C⟩ **7** Starch reacts slowly with water to form sugars. A student suspects that the reaction could be speeded up using enzymes. To test this idea the student measured 10 cm³ 1% starch solution into each of four test tubes. To three of these she added 1 cm³ of solutions of three enzymes. Each enzyme solution was of the same concentration. The fourth test tube had 1 cm³ of water added to it. The test tubes were kept at 25 °C. Samples were removed from the tubes at two-minute intervals to test whether starch was present. The results are shown in the table below.

Test Tube	Time from start (min)	0	2	4	6	8	10	12	14	16
1	10 cm³ starch + 1 cm³ enzyme 1	✓	✓	✓	✓	✓	✓	✓	✓	✓
2	10 cm³ starch + 1 cm³ enzyme 2	✓	✓	✓	✗	✗	✗	✗	✗	✗
3	10 cm³ starch + 1 cm³ enzyme 3	✓	✓	✓	✓	✓	✓	✗	✗	✗
4	10 cm³ starch + 1 cm³ water	✓	✓	✓	✓	✓	✓	✓	✓	✓

✓ = starch present   ✗ = starch absent

(a) What piece of apparatus should be used to measure out 1 cm³ of enzyme solution? *Skill (b)*

(b) How could the test tubes be kept at 25 °C for 16 minutes if the room temperature is 20 °C? *Skill (b)*

(c) What was the purpose of test tube 4 in this experiment? *Skill (f)*

(d) Which enzyme was the most effective at speeding up the reaction between starch and water? *Skill (e)*

(e) The student has previously learnt that chemical reactions are speeded up by raising the temperature. She wanted to see whether this was also true when an enzyme was used in a chemical reaction.

10 cm³ of 1% starch solution was measured into each of seven test tubes, together with 1 cm³ of a solution of enzyme 2. The test tubes were kept at temperatures between 10 °C and 60 °C and tested every two minutes to see when all of the starch had been broken down. The results are shown in the table below.

Time from start (min)	0	2	4	6	8	10	12	14	16	18
10 °C	✓	✓	✓	✓	✓	✓	✓	✓	✗	✗
20 °C	✓	✓	✓	✓	✗	✗	✗	✗	✗	✗
30 °C	✓	✓	✗	✗	✗	✗	✗	✗	✗	✗
40 °C	✓	✗	✗	✗	✗	✗	✗	✗	✗	✗
50°	✓	✓	✓	✓	✓	✓	✓	✓	✗	✗
60°	✓	✓	✓	✓	✓	✓	✓	✓	✓	✓

✓ = starch present   ✗ = starch absent

(i) On a grid like Figure 5.8, plot a graph of the time taken to break down the starch (y-axis) against temperature (x-axis). *Skill (d)*

$$(NH_4)_2SO_4(s) + Ca(OH)_2(s) \rightarrow 2NH_3(g) + CaSO_4(s) + 2H_2O(l)$$

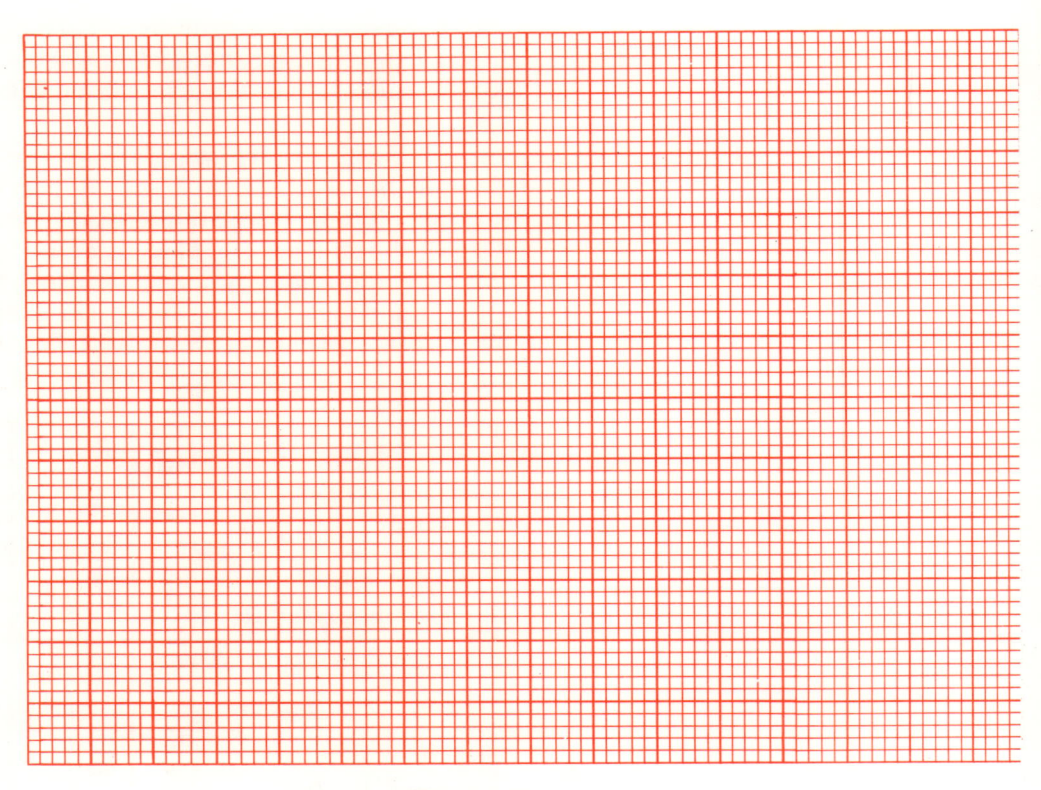

Fig. 5.8 The graph

(ii) Describe fully the effect of temperature on the rate of reaction involving this enzyme.
Skill (e)

(f) The student has previously learnt that increasing the concentration of reacting substances in a reaction will increase the rate of reaction.

Describe carefully, giving full details, how the student should find out whether changes in enzyme 2 concentration alters the rate of reaction.
Skill (f)

(g) Starch can also be broken down by boiling it with dilute hydrochloric acid. Draw a labelled diagram of apparatus which could be used to boil 25 cm³ of a starch/hydrochloric acid mixture for 20 minutes. Your apparatus should not allow the mixture to boil dry.
Skill (f)

8 You are asked to design an experiment to test whether wet clothing is as good a heat insulator as dry clothing. The equipment you can use is shown in Figure 5.9.

Think about how you would do the experiment and then present your design using the following plan:

(a) A diagram of your experiment set up.
(b) A few sentences to outline the procedure which you intend to adopt. Include any safety precautions and steps which you would take to ensure reliability of your results.
(c) A statement of any measurements and readings which you would take.
(d) How you would interpret your readings to reach a conclusion.
Skills (b) and (f)

9 Ammonium sulphate is used as a fertilizer to supply nitrogen to plants. When ammonium sulphate is heated with an alkali, such as calcium hydroxide, ammonia gas is formed. Water and calcium sulphate are also formed. The equation for the reaction is:

$$(NH_4)_2SO_4(s) + Ca(OH)_2(s) \rightarrow 2NH_3(g) + CaSO_4(s) + 2H_2O(l)$$

Shiny copper beaker

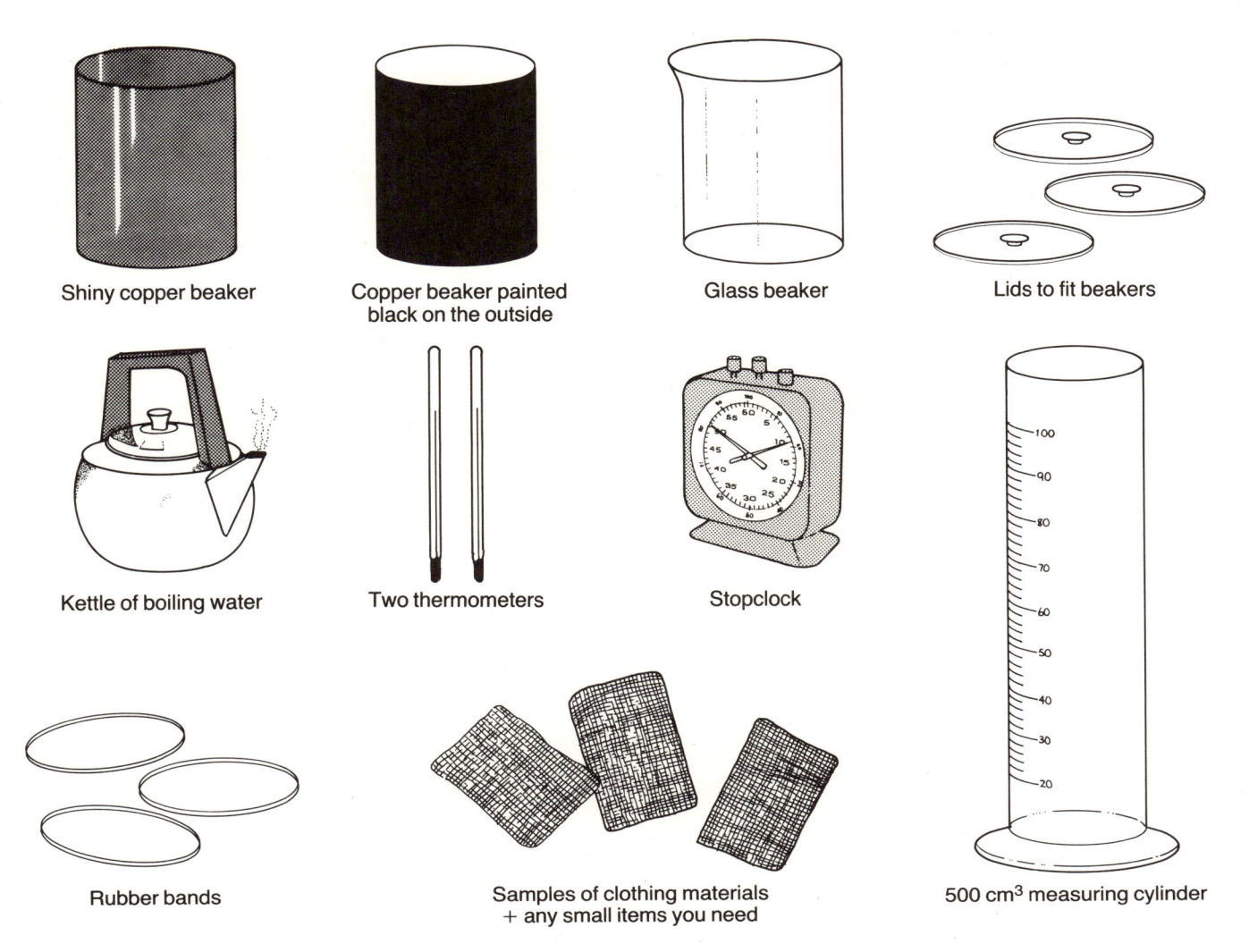

Copper beaker painted black on the outside

Glass beaker

Lids to fit beakers

Kettle of boiling water

Two thermometers

Stopclock

Rubber bands

Samples of clothing materials + any small items you need

500 cm³ measuring cylinder

Fig. 5.9 The equipment

Ammonia is very soluble in water. It can be dried by passing it through lumps of calcium oxide.

(a) Figure 5.10 shows a diagram of apparatus set up for an experiment to find the volume of ammonia gas produced when 0.1 g of ammonium sulphate is heated with excess calcium hydroxide. Suggest one change which must be made before any ammonia gas can be collected. *Skill (g)*

Gas syringe

Mixture of ammonium sulphate and calcium hydroxide

U-tube

Calcium oxide granules

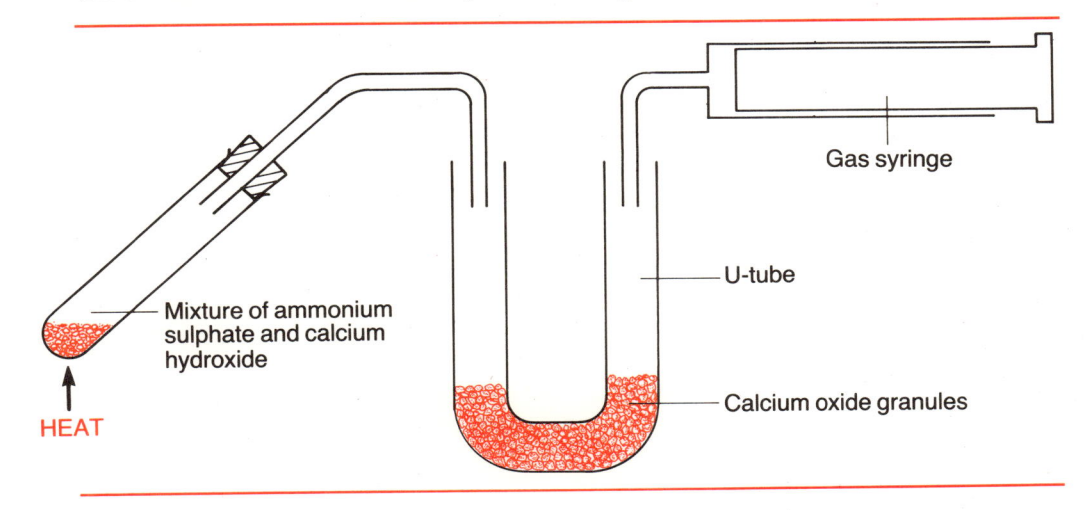

HEAT

Fig. 5.10 The apparatus

(b) Why is it better to use calcium oxide lumps rather than calcium powder to dry the gas? *Skill (g)*

(c) Frequently, even when the experiment is carried out in suitable apparatus, less ammonia gas is collected than expected. Why is some ammonia gas 'lost'? *Skill (f)*

(d) Some fertilizers need to be very soluble in water to be quick-acting. Other fertilizers are less soluble and act over a longer period. Factors which affect the speed of dissolving in water include:
- the size of the crystals
- the temperature of the water
- the mass of fertilizer
- the method of stirring
- the volume of water.

Describe carefully an experiment which you could use to find out which of two solid fertilizers dissolves faster. *Skill (f)*

⬥S⬥ ⬥B⬥ **10** This question refers to the subject of osmosis.

Three cylinders (diameter 0.5 cm) were cut from a potato, with a cork borer. They were then put into separate test tubes and each covered with a measured volume of one of the following liquids.
Test tube 1 distilled water
Test tube 2 sucrose solution (8.5%)
Test tube 3 sucrose solution (17%)
At the start of the experiment all three cylinders were 5 cm long. Figure 5.11 shows the cylinders after they had been in the test tubes for 24 hours.

Fig. 5.11 The cylinders after 24 hours

(a) Measure the length of each potato cylinder and complete the following table.

Potato cylinder	Original length (in mm)	Final length (in mm)	Change in length (in mm)
1	50		
2	50		
3	50		

Skills (c) and (d)

(b) Explain the changes in length in cylinders 1 and 3. *Skill (e)*

(c) What would have happened to the concentration of the sucrose solution in test tube 3 after 24 hours? *Skill (e)*

(d) Why is there no change in length in cylinder 2? *Skill (e)*

(e) Suggest another method which could be used to show the changes which occurred in the potato cylinders. *Skill (f)*

⬥S⬥ ⬥P⬥ **11** Sarah is investigating the stretchiness of some nylon fishing line. She uses the experiment set up in Figure 5.12.

Each time she adds an extra 1 N force she records the scale reading next to the pointer. These are shown in the diagrams in Figure 5.13.

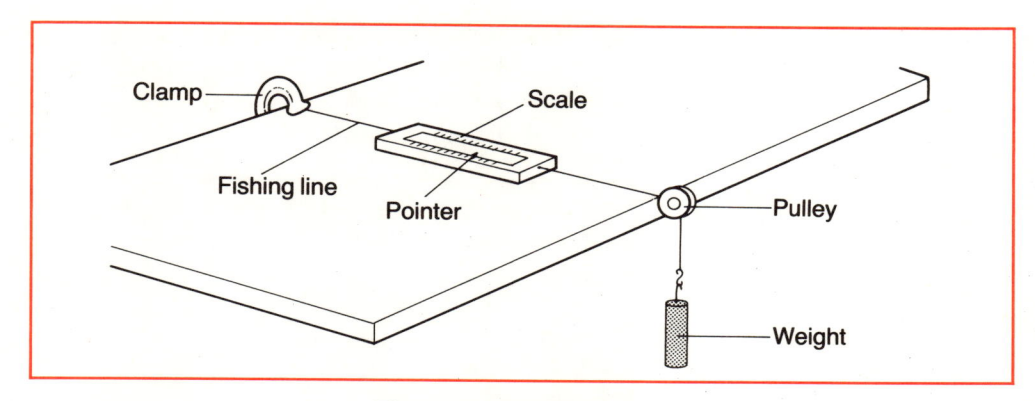

Fig. 5.12 The experiment

Force = 1 N
Scale reading =

Force = 2 N
Scale reading =

Force = 3 N
Scale reading =

Force = 4 N
Scale reading =

Force = 5 N
Scale reading =

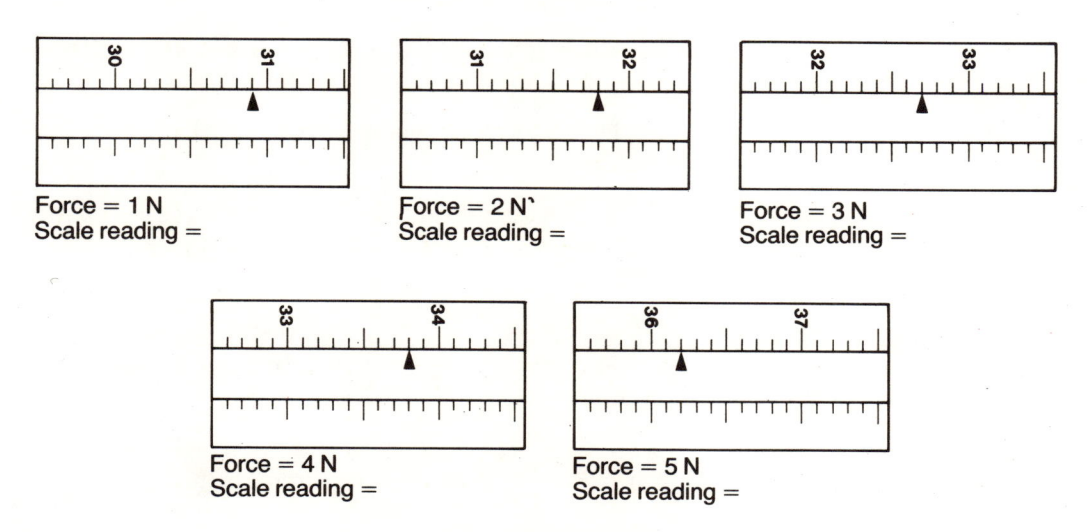

Fig. 5.13 The results

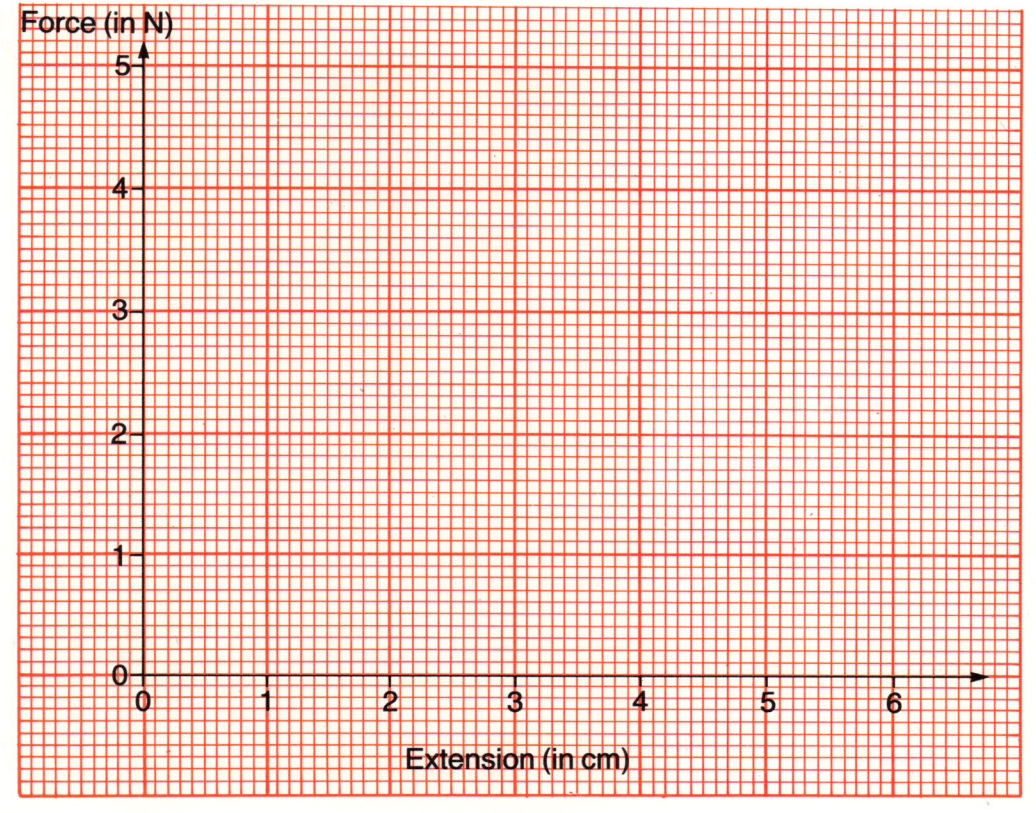

Fig. 5.14 The graph

(a) Record the scale readings in the spaces provided. By subtracting the original length (30.0 cm) from each reading you can now work out the extension in each case.
Complete the following table.

Weight added (in N)	Extension (in cm)
0	0.0
1	
2	
3	
4	
5	

Skills (c) and (d)

(b) Use a grid like Figure. 5.14 to plot a graph of force (in N) on the *y*-axis against extension (in cm) on the *x*-axis. *Skill (d)*

(c) Does the extension go up in equal sized jumps each time another 1 N force is added? *Skill (e)*

(d) Sarah found that the breaking force of the line was between 7 N and 8 N. How could she adapt the experiment to try to measure this force more precisely? *Skill (g)*

S C **12** Malachite is a mineral containing copper(II) carbonate. An investigation was carried out to find out what fraction of the mineral is copper.

> **Stage 1** The mass of the sample of malachite was found.
> **Stage 2** Dilute sulphuric acid was added to the mineral until all of the copper(II) carbonate had reacted. Carbon dioxide and blue copper(II) sulphate solution was formed.
> **Stage 3** The copper(II) sulphate solution was separated from the mineral which had not reacted with the acid.
> **Stage 4** The copper(II) sulphate solution was electrolysed using a copper cathode (negative electrode), a carbon anode (positive electrode) and a current of 0.1 A (Figure 5.15).
> **Stage 5** When all the copper had been deposited the copper cathode was rinsed with distilled water, dried and the mass of the copper cathode found.

(a) In Stage 2, give two ways of making the mineral react faster without increasing the concentration of the acid. *Skill (g)*

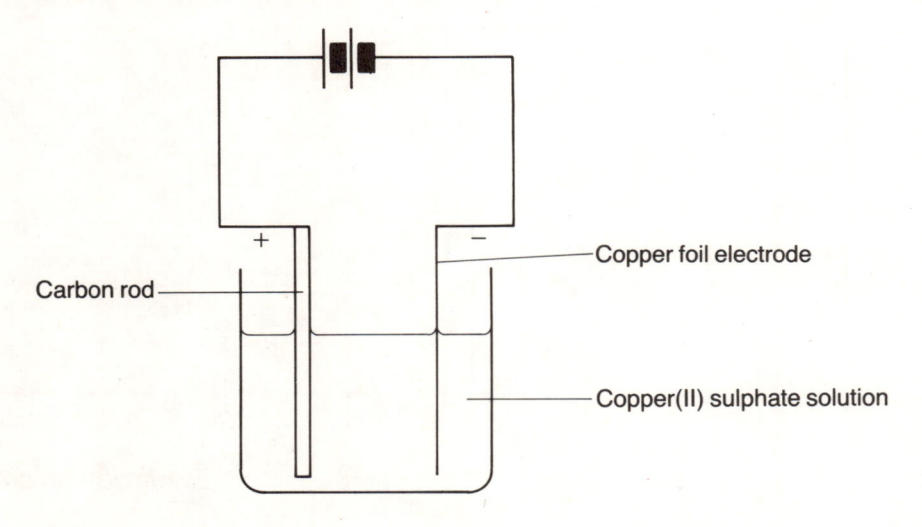

Fig. 5.15 The circuit

(b) In Stage 2, how will you know that no more copper(II) carbonate is left to react? *Skill (c)*

(c) How would you carry out the separation process in Stage 3? *Skill (f)*

(d) Apart from the apparatus in Figure 5.15, what other apparatus would be required for Stages 4 and 5? *Skill (b)*

(e) List the measurements or readings that would have to be made to work out how much copper had been deposited on the copper cathode. *Skill (f)*

(f) How would you know that all the copper from the copper(II) sulphate solution had been deposited onto the cathode? *Skill (f)*

(g) The results of the class are shown in the table below.

Group	Mass of mineral used (in g)	Mass of copper formed (in g)
1	15.0	0.60
2	30.0	1.40
3	45.0	2.25
4	50.0	2.60
5	60.0	

The results of the class were plotted on the grid which is shown in Figure 5.16.

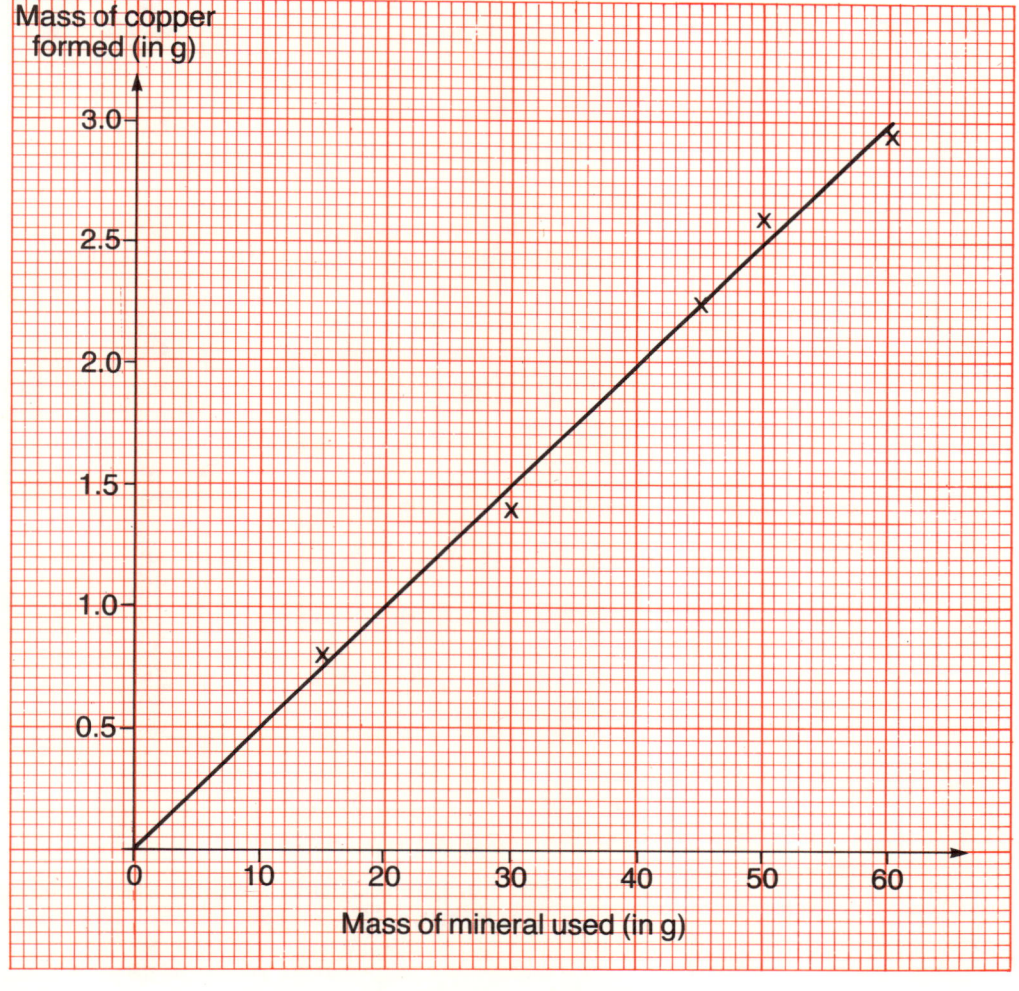

Fig. 5.16 The results graph

(i) What mass of copper was formed by the group which used 60.0 g of the mineral? *Skill (e)*

(ii) Use the graph to predict what mass of copper would be present in 40.0 g of the mineral. *Skill (e)*

(iii) Use your answer to **(g)** *(ii)* to calculate the percentage of copper in the ore. *Skill (e)*

(iv) Why do the points not all lie on a straight line? *Skill (e)*

◇S◇ ◇C◇ **13** This is an investigation of the rate of reaction between magnesium and hydrochloric acid.

$Mg(s) + 2HCl(aq) \rightarrow MgCl_2(aq) + H_2(g)$

(a) Using the apparatus shown in Figure 5.17, draw a diagram of apparatus set up to collect the volume of hydrogen produced at regular intervals. You should include in your diagram a method enabling you to start the reaction when you are ready. *Skill (f)*

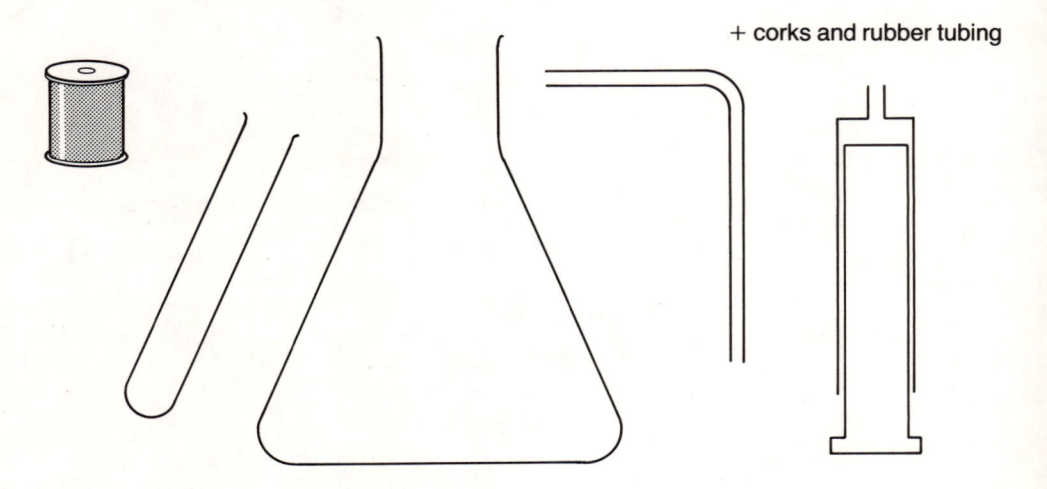

+ corks and rubber tubing

Fig. 17 The apparatus

(b) The tables below include the results of two experiments.

Experiment 1

Time (in s)	Volume of gas (in cm^3)
0	0
10	40
20	57
30	65
40	69
50	70
60	70
70	70
80	70

Experiment 2

Time (in s)	Volume of gas (in cm^3)
0	0
10	17
20	30
30	42
40	52
50	59
60	65
70	68
80	70
90	70

(i) Plot these results on a grid like Figure 5.18, using one set of axes. Draw two graphs and label them 1 and 2. *Skill (e)*

(ii) From your graph, find the volume of gas which would be collected in experiment 1 after 15 seconds. *Skill (e)*

(c) In these two experiments equal masses of magnesium ribbon were used. In each experiment, 25 cm^3 of hydrochloric acid were used.

However, in one case a small volume of water was added to the acid before the experiment was started.

(i) How is it possible to get two pieces of magnesium ribbon of equal mass without weighing? *Skill (f)*

(ii) In which experiment was the water added to the acid? Explain your answer. *Skill (e)*

(d) The experiment was repeated with the undiluted acid and magnesium powder. The mass of magnesium powder used was half the mass of magnesium ribbon used in the previous experiments. On a grid like Figure 5.18, sketch the graph you would expect for this experiment.
Skill (e)

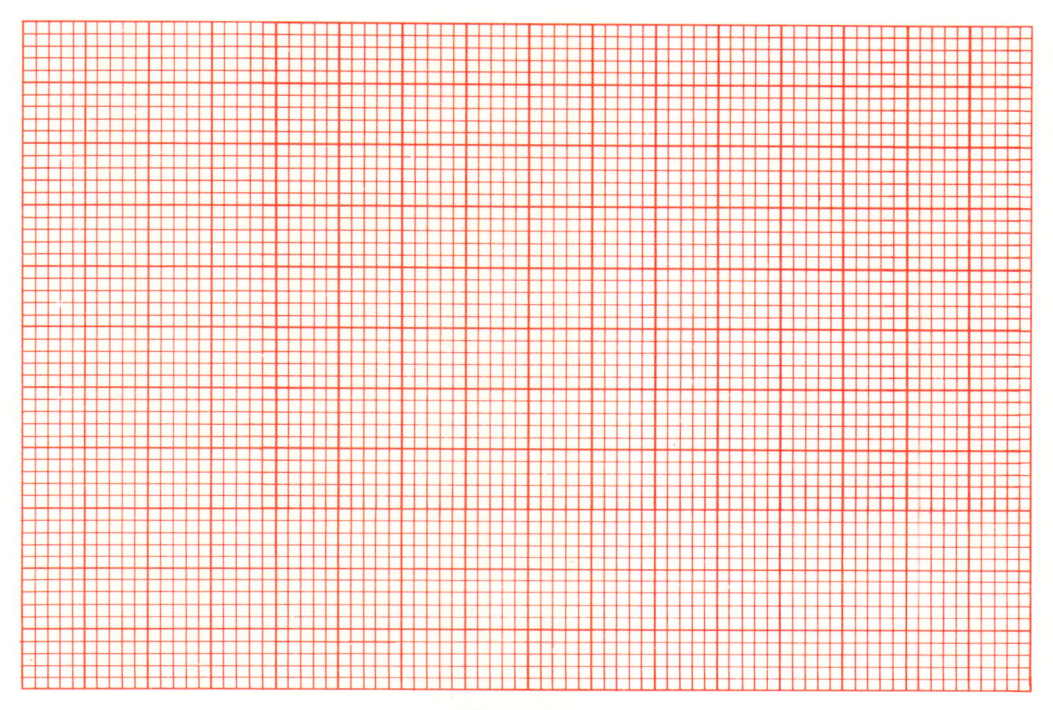

Fig. 5.18

⟨S⟩ ⟨P⟩ **14** Figure 5.19 shows an experiment which is used to show the behaviour of light striking a plane (flat) mirror.

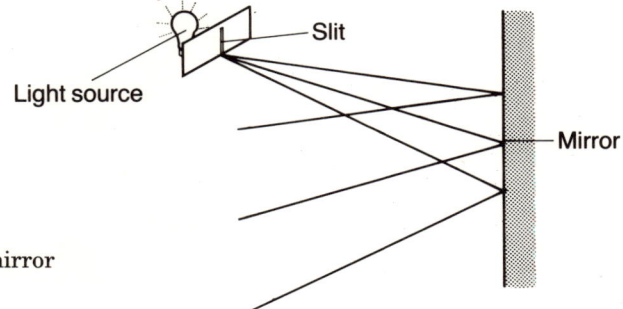

Fig. 5.19 Light striking a plane mirror

Elizabeth marks the position of the back of the mirror with a straight line. She then uses two dots to mark each ray of light before it hits the mirror, and two crosses to mark the position of the reflected ray. She removes the lamp and the mirror and joins the first pair of dots with a straight line. She does the same to the pair of crosses which represent the reflected ray. Her piece of paper then looks like Figure 5.20.

Notice that she has drawn in a 'normal' line where the ray hits the mirror. This is a line drawn at 90° to the mirror surface. The angle of incidence is the angle between the incident (incoming) ray and the normal line. The angle of reflection is the angle between the reflected ray and the normal line.

(a) Complete the diagram by drawing in the other two rays before and after they hit the mirror. Each pair of dots and crosses has been given a different number so that you can identify them. *Skill (d)*

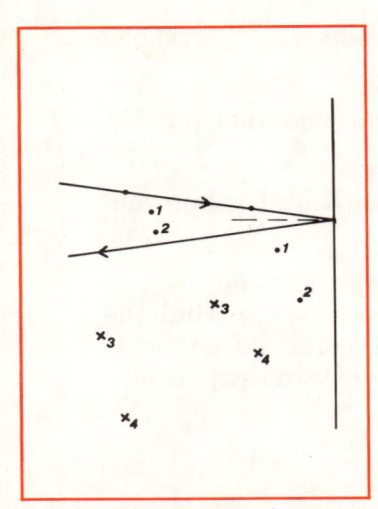

Fig. 5.20 Elizabeth's results

(b) For each ray, measure the angle of incidence and the angle of reflection. Record your results in a table like the one below.

	Angle of incidence	Angle of reflection
ray 1 ray 2 ray 3		

Skills (c) and (d)

(c) Look at the pattern of the results in the table. Can you draw a simple conclusion about the way each pair of angles is related? *Skill (e)*

(d) Can you think of any reasons why not *every* pair of results may exactly fit your conclusion? Can you suggest any improvements which might lead to better results? *Skill (g)*

(e) Now concentrate on the reflected rays **only**. Suppose an eye were looking at these rays. The eye-brain system would assume that the light had travelled in straight lines. Trace the reflected rays back *behind the mirror* (use dotted lines) to find where they appear to have come from. This is called the image point. Use solid lines to trace back the incident rays. The place where these cross is the lamp position. Compare the lamp position with the image position. What conclusion can you make about these two positions? *Skills (c) and (e)*

(f) You are at the back of a crowd with a long cardboard tube, two mirrors, scissors and sticky tape. Draw a diagram of a piece of equipment which you could use to see over the crowd. *Skill (f)*

⟨S⟩ ⟨B⟩ **15** Figure 5.21 shows the stages in the growth of a locust. A locust hatches into the first nymph stage (a), it moults at intervals to go through four more nymphal stages, (b) to (e). It then moults to form adult (f).
A locust hatched on 2 April. It moulted on the following dates:
7, 11, 15, 20, 28 April.
The length of the animal remains the same between moults.

(a) Measure the length of the animals as shown in Figure 5.21. Taking the length from the tip of the abdomen to the front of the head (exclude the length of the antennae). Note the scale for each stage. *Skill (c)*

(b) Record the **actual** length of the locust in the following table.

Date	Length (in mm)
2 April 7 April 11 April 15 April 20 April 28 April	

Skill (d)

(c) Plot the length of the body of the locust from 2 April to 30 April on a grid like Figure 5.22. *Skill (d)*

(d) Why does the locust grow in stages? *Skill (e)*

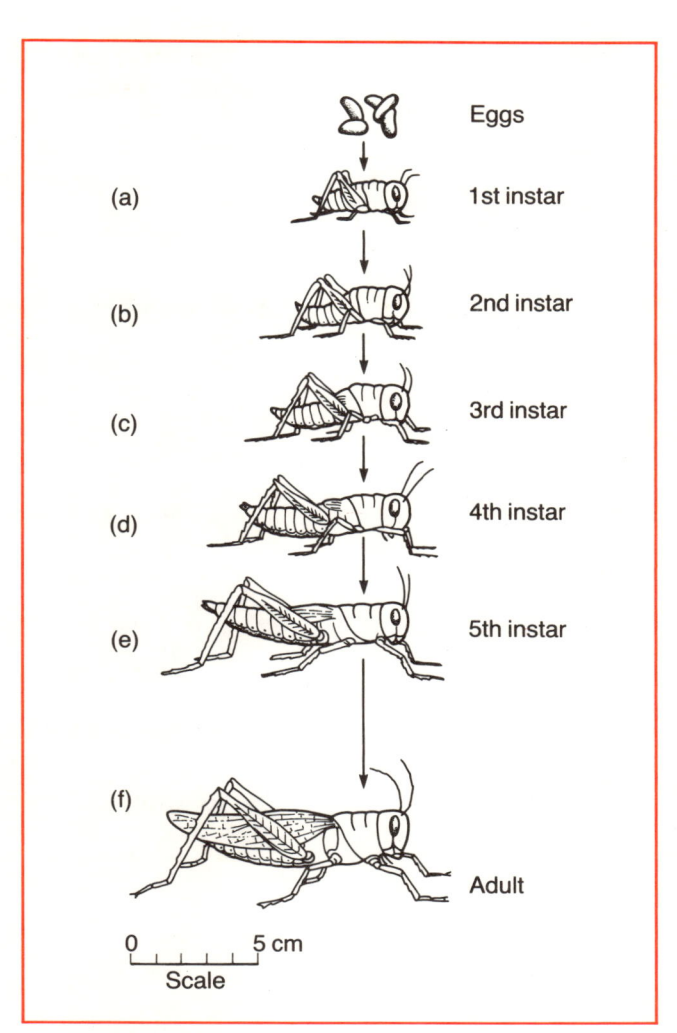

Fig. 5.21 Stages in the development of a locust

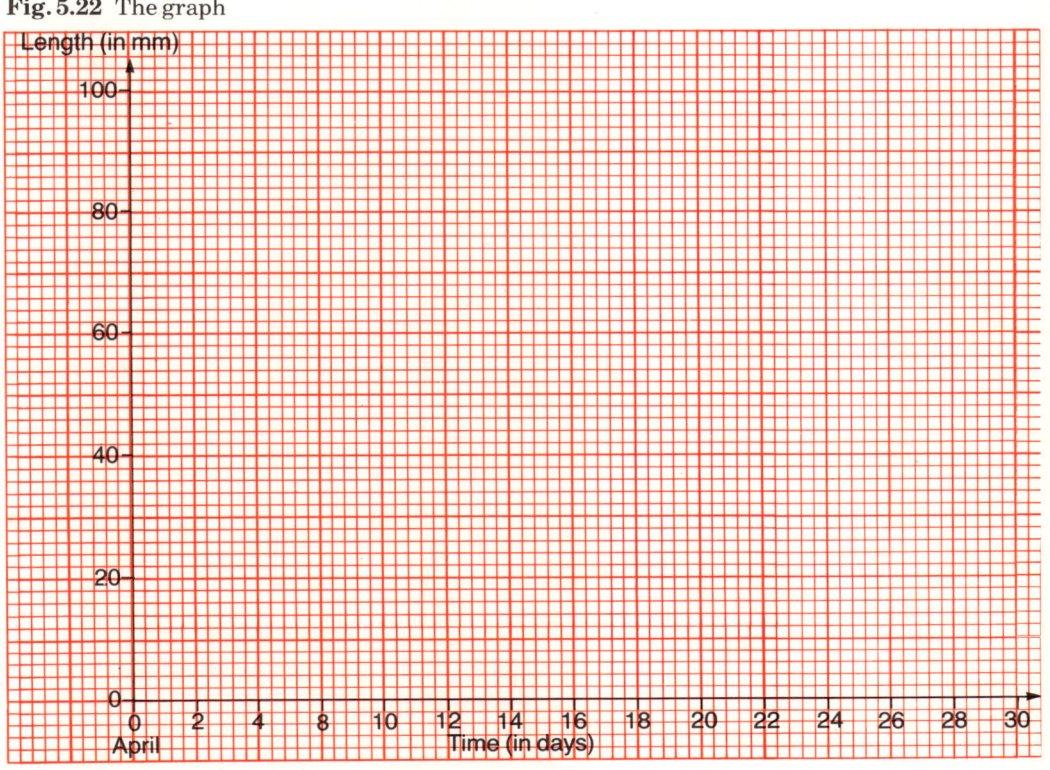

Fig. 5.22 The graph

(e) List six other features which could be measured to show the growth of a locust. *Skill (f)*

(f) List two factors which might affect the rate of growth of a locust. *Skill (f)*

16 Ten cress seeds were germinated on damp blotting paper and then kept in the dark. Ten more were germinated but then kept continuously in the light. Both groups were left for a week in identical conditions except for the light. After a week the lengths of the roots and shoots were measured and recorded. The results are shown in the tables below.

Seedlings grown in the light

Seed number	Shoot length (in mm)	Root length (in mm)
1	22	55
2	20	45
3	25	47
4	25	45
5	23	42
6	24	50
7	20	37
8	31	43
9	31	45
10	27	50

Seedlings grown in the dark

Seed number	Shoot length (in mm)	Root length (in mm)
1	32	56
2	24	40
3	35	44
4	42	54
5	43	53
6	32	45
7	31	47
8	37	50
9	27	31
10	34	54

(a) Calculate the average shoot length and the average root length for both treatments and put your answers in a table. *Skill (d)*

(b) What is the effect of light on shoot growth? *Skill (e)*

(c) What is the effect of light on root growth? *Skill (e)*

(d) Figure 5.23 shows two of these seedlings. A was grown in the light, B in the dark.
Observe and measure the differences between them and record these in a suitable table. *Skills (c) and (d)*

(e) Plants grown on a windowsill bend towards the light. Devise an experiment to show that light from one side causes bending in cress seedlings. *Skill (f)*

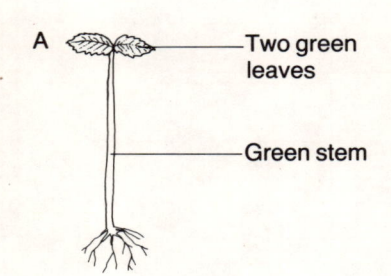

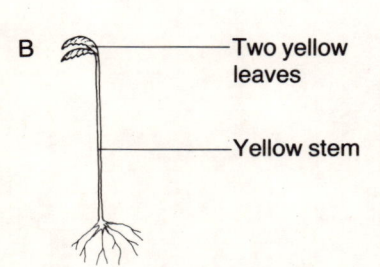

Fig. 5.23 Two seedlings

A — Two green leaves, Green stem
B — Two yellow leaves, Yellow stem

17 Oxygen gas is slightly denser than air and slightly soluble in water. It can be prepared by adding a solution of hydrogen peroxide in water to manganese(IV) oxide, a black solid.

(a) Copy and complete Figure 5.24 to show apparatus which could be used to prepare and collect several test tubes filled with oxygen gas. *Skills (b) and (f)*

(b) Explain how you would ensure that there was no air in the oxygen collected. *Skill (g)*

Fig. 5.24 (Flask containing Manganese(IV) oxide)

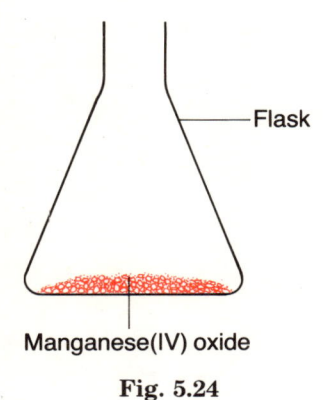

(c) Six elements were heated on burning spoons and plunged into separate test tubes of oxygen. Universal indicator solution was shaken up with the oxide formed in each case. The observations are recorded in Figure 5.25.

Element	metal/ non-metal	Reaction with oxygen/ appearance of oxide	Colour formed in solution with Universal Indicator	pH of solution	Acidity/ alkalinity of solution
A	metal	glows brightly, forms white ash	blue/green		
B	metal	no glow or flame, forms black solid	green		
C	non-metal	sparkles, forms a colourless gas	orange		
D	metal	burst violently into flames, forms white ash	violet		
E	non-metal	bursts into flames, forms steamy gas	red		
F	metal	burns vigorously, forms white ash	blue		

Fig. 5.25 A student's results table

(i) Comment on the difference in the appearance of the oxides formed from metals and non metals. *Skill (e)*

Here is some information about the colours of Universal indicator in solutions of different pH.

pH	Colour	Acid or alkali
1–3	red	strong acid
4	pink	
5	orange	
6	yellow	
7	green	neutral
8	green-blue	
9	blue	
10	blue-violet	
11–14	violet	strong alkali

(ii) Draw a table including the pH of each solution formed and the acidity/ alkalinity the pH indicates. *Skill (d)*

(iii) Copy and complete the table below to summarize the properties of the oxides of metals and non-metals.

	pH of solution of oxides	Acidity/alkalinity of solution of oxides
metals non metals		

Skill (e)

(iv) Put the metals in order of their reactivity with oxygen. Put the most reactive metal first. *Skill (e)*

(v) Comment on the connection between the reactivity of the metal and the pH of the oxide formed. *Skill (e)*

18 You are asked to carry out an investigation to find out whether washing powder X, which contains an enzyme, is better for removing grass stains than washing powder Y which does not contain an enzyme.

(a) List three factors which you would have to keep constant in order to compare the two washing powders fairly. *Skill (f)*

(b) List the apparatus that you would need for your investigation. *Skill (b)*

(c) Briefly outline the steps you would take to carry out your investigation. *Skill (f)*

19 A student made drawings of the pattern of colouring on two leaves, A and B, on a potted plant. These are shown in Figure 5.26.

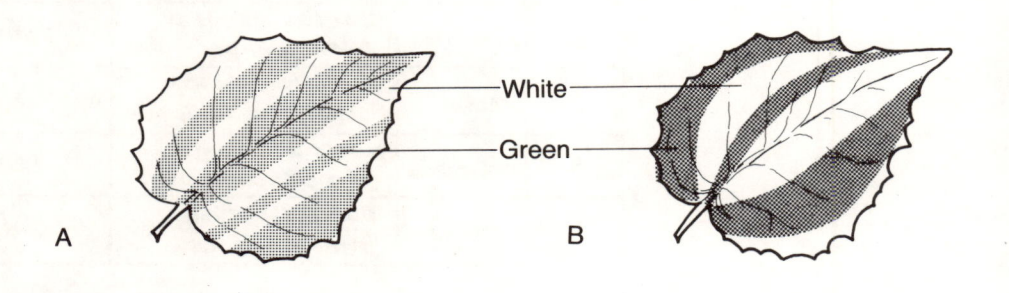

Fig. 5.26 Leaves on a potted plant

The potted plant was put in darkness for a week. Leaf A was then covered with black paper and the plant was left in bright light for eight hours. After this, the two leaves were removed and tested for the presence of starch. The results are shown in Figure 5.27.

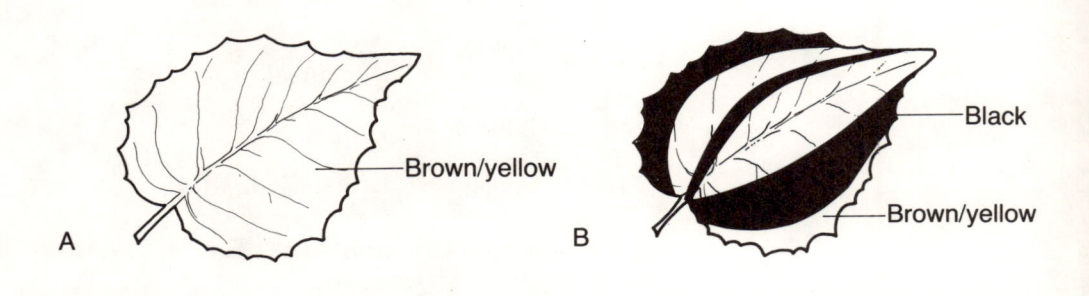

Fig. 5.27 The results

(a) Explain why the plant was put into the dark for a week. *Skill (g)*

(b) The leaves were boiled in ethanol before the starch test was done. Explain how you would do this safely. *Skill (b)*

(c) How would you carry out the test for starch? *Skill (b)*

(d) What conclusions can be drawn from the results of this investigation? *Skill (e)*

20 You are asked to test which of the following:
10 g of wood
10 g of coal
10 g of oil
gives out the greatest amount of heat energy when burned.

Assume that you have all the apparatus of your school laboratory available, and use this outline.
(a) Diagram of the experiment set-up.
(b) The procedure you would use including safety precautions.
(c) Any measurements or readings you would take. How you would interpret your results.

Skill (f)

S B C 21 Here are some instructions for making a simple fermenter.

> (1) Sterilize all equipment to be used with a solution made by dissolving a Camden tablet in water. Camden tablets release sulphur dioxide when dissolved in water.
> (2) Dissolve 20 g of sugar in 1 dm^3 of water.
> (3) Boil the sugar solution and leave it to cool.
> (4) Add 2 g of yeast to 10 cm^3 of water.
> (5) Add to this yeast suspension some yeast nutrients including some ammonium salts.
> (6) Mix the yeast suspension with sugar solution and pour the mixture into the sterilized bottle.
> (7) Put an airlock into the bung and put this into the neck of the bottle. Make sure it fits tightly.
> (8) Place the bottle in a warm place.

The fermenter is shown in Figure 5.28.

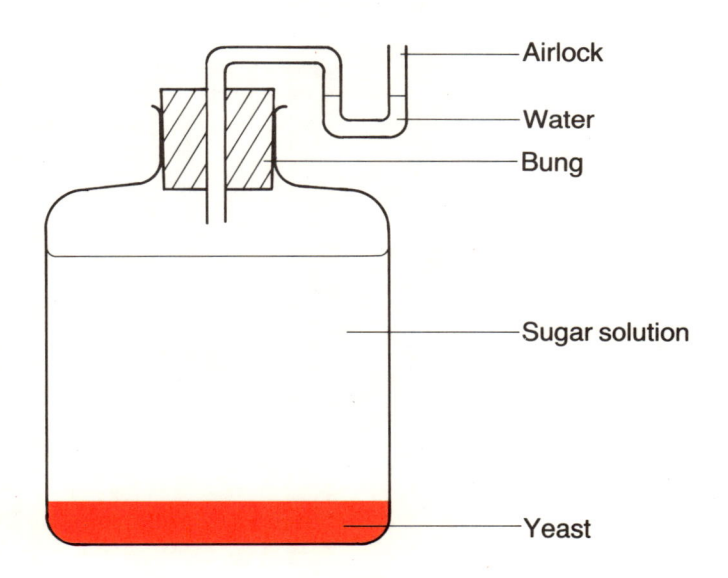

Fig. 5.28 The fermenter

(a) Why is it necessary to sterilize all the equipment? *Skill (b)*

(b) Why is the sugar solution boiled and then cooled? *Skill (b)*

(c) Why is sugar solution used in the fermenter? *Skill (b)*

(d) Why must the bottle not be kept completely airtight? *Skill (b)*

(e) Why is an airlock with water necessary? *Skill (b)*

(f) How would you modify the apparatus to test the carbon dioxide gas produced? *Skill (f)*

(g) Why is the fermenter placed in a warm place? *Skill (b)*

22 This question is about an experiment to find the current gain (amplification) of a transistor. Figure 5.29 shows part of the circuit to be used. The base, collector and emitter terminals have been labelled with their initial letters.

(a) Add the following to the circuit diagram:

A milliammeter —(mA)— to measure the current in the base lead.

An ammeter —(A)— to measure the current in the collector lead.
Skill (b)

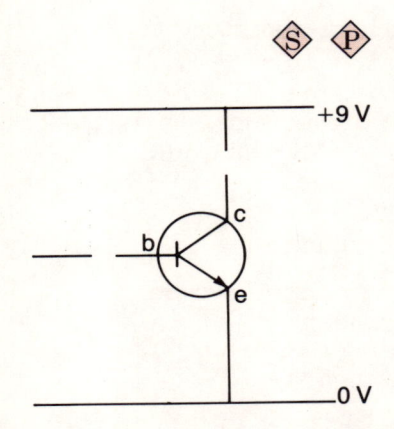

Fig. 5.29 Part of the circuit

(b) A student measured the collector current for a range of different base currents. His results are shown in the following table.

Collector current (in A)	Base current (in mA)
0.10	5
0.24	11
0.39	20
0.70	28
0.72	36
0.80	42
0.80	50
0.80	58

Use a grid like Figure 5.30 to plot a graph of collector current (up) against base current (across). Which pair of readings looks wrong? Ignore this point when drawing in the best line. *Skill (d)*

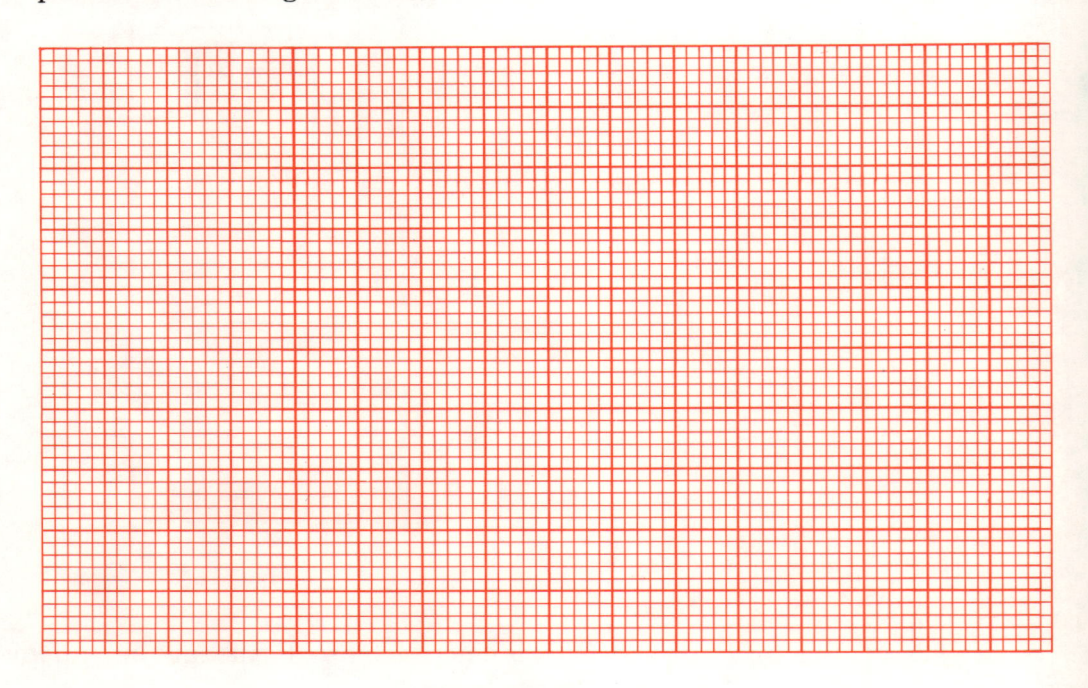

Fig. 5.30 The grid

(c) The student plans to use a warning lamp in the collector circuit. The current in the lamp is 0.67 A. Find the current in the base when the lamp is operating normally. *Skill (e)*

(d) Ignoring the pair of results where an error has been made, calculate the current gain for each set of readings.
Use this equation.

current gain = collector current ÷ base current

Don't forget that the readings of base current are in mA.

$1 \text{ mA} = \frac{1}{1000} \text{ A} = 0.001 \text{ A} = 10^{-3} \text{A}$

One set is done here as an example:
 collector current = 0.39 A   base current = 20 mA
 current gain = $0.39 \div (20 \times 10^{-3})$
              = 19.5 *Skill (e)*

(e) Write a short conclusion about the way in which the current gain of the transistor changes as the base and collector current increase. *Skill (e)*

S P

23 You are provided with the items in Figure 5.31.

Using as many or as few of these items as you need, describe an experiment which you could do to find the average volume of one screw. You might find it easier to describe your procedure with a series of sketches, to be followed by a few sentences to describe the way in which you would achieve your final answer. *Skill (f)*

S P

24 Tracey is doing an experiment which compares different ways of loading heavy objects onto a van. She first of all lifts a brick vertically up through a height of 0.8 m.

(a) Write down the reading on the forcemeter in Figure 5.32(a). Use the equation

change in gravitational potential energy
    = weight × change in height

to find the amount of energy (in joules) gained by the brick. *Skill (c)*

(b) She now does the same job by pulling the brick up a slope. She uses a smaller force but the distance she pulls the brick is now 2.2 m. Write down the reading on the forcemeter in Figure 5.32(b).

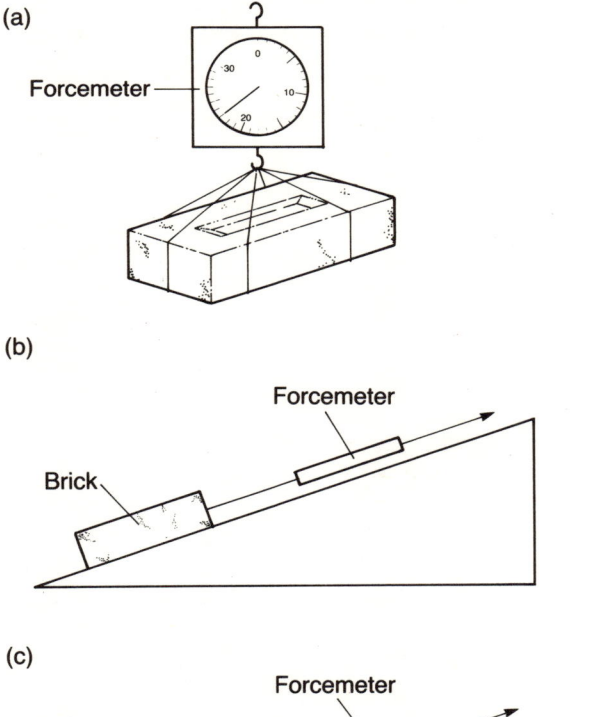

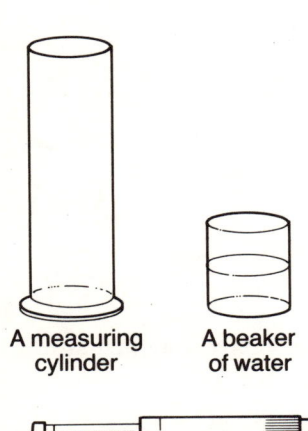

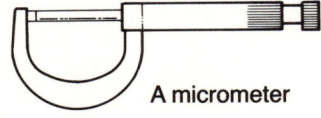

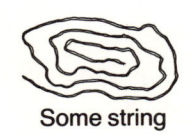

Fig. 5.31 The equipment

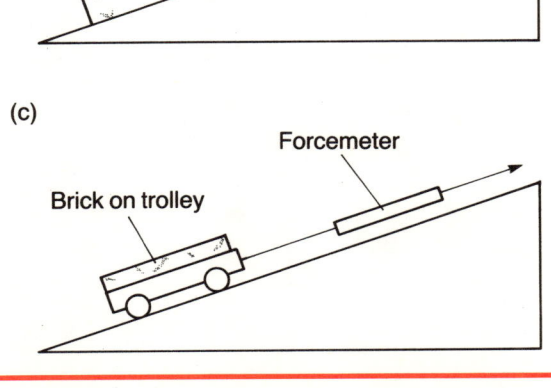

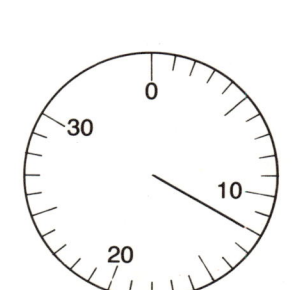

Fig. 5.32 (a), (b) and (c)

Use the equation

energy used = force × distance it moves

to find the energy she uses in pulling the brick up the slope.
Is this more than, less than or the same as the energy gained by the brick?
Where do you think the rest of the energy has gone? *Skills (c), (d) and (e)*

(c) The efficiency of a method of doing a job is defined as being the useful energy output divided by the total energy input. In this case it is
g.p.e. gained by brick ÷ energy used by Tracey.
Find the efficiency of this way of getting the heavy object onto the van.
Skill (e)

(d) Tracey then puts the brick onto a small trolley and pulls it up the slope.
Write down the reading on the forcemeter in Figure 5.32(c). *Skill (c)*

(e) The distance is the same as before (2.2 m). Find the energy she uses to pull the brick and trolley up. Work out the efficiency of this method.
Skill (e)

(f) Which of the last two methods is more efficient? Why do you think this is? *Skill (f)*

25 Two students, Tom and Jerry, noticed that bubbles of air appeared on the inside of a beaker of water when it was stood in sunlight.

Tom formed the hypothesis that heat in the sun's rays warms the water and that air is less soluble, the warmer the water becomes.

Jerry formed the hypothesis that it is the light which provides the energy for the air to escape from the water. The longer the light shines on the water the more air escapes.

Devise experiments to test the two hypotheses. *Skill (f)*

26 Figure 5.33 shows a simple flowchart which can be used to identify four colourless gases.
A colourless gas, labelled P, puts out a lighted splint.
(a) Which two gases could gas P be? *Skill (a)*

(b) Draw a diagram to show how you would now test this gas to identify it. *Skills (a) and (f)*

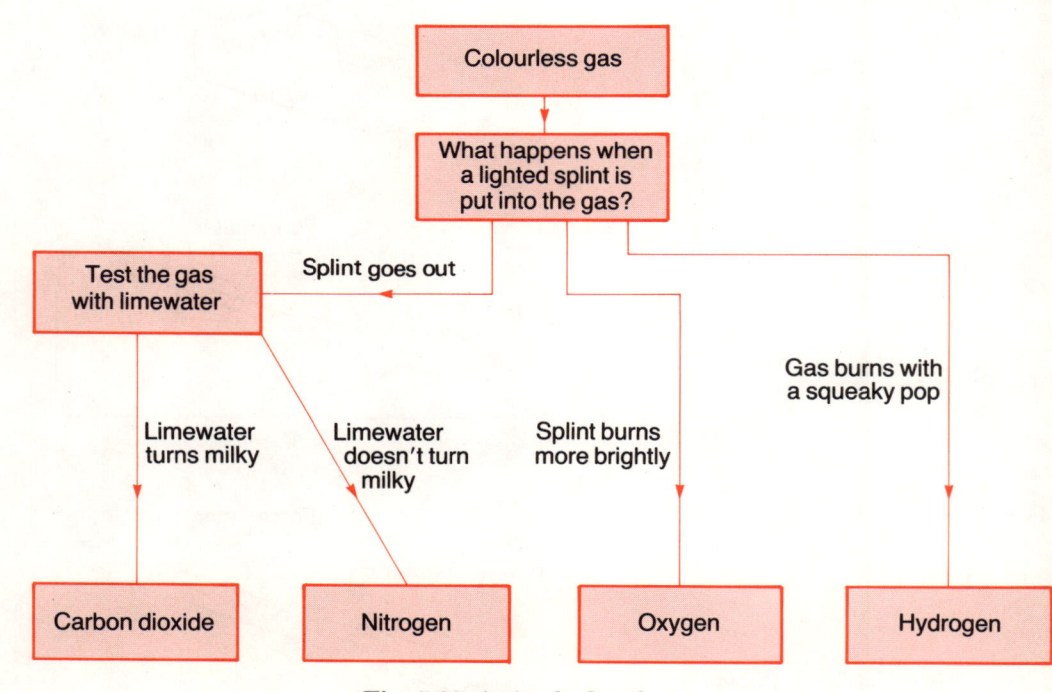

Fig. 5.33 A simple flowchart

27 When pondweed is illuminated, bubbles of oxygen are released into the water. Figure 5.34 shows the apparatus used to investigate the rate at which oxygen is produced at different light intensities.

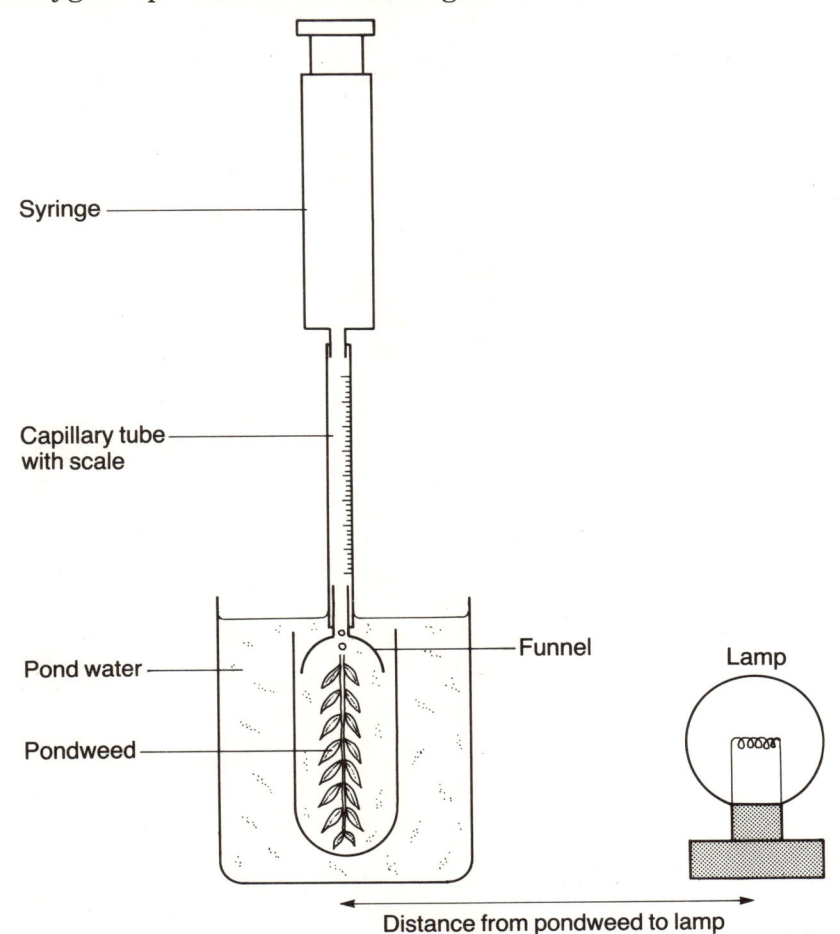

Fig. 5.34 The apparatus

As oxygen is produced it collects in the funnel. After five minutes the oxygen is drawn into the narrow capillary tube with the syringe. The volume can be measured on the scale.

To reduce the light intensity the lamp is moved away from the beaker containing the pondweed.

The table below shows the result of one investigation.

Distance from lamp to pondweed (in cm)	Volume of oxygen produced in 5 minutes (in mm^3)
5	240
10	54
15	28
20	12
25	7
30	2

(a) Before beginning the investigation air is bubbled through the pondwater. Explain why. *Skill (f)*

(b) Carbon dioxide is provided in the pondwater by adding a solution of sodium hydrogencarbonate. Explain the purpose of the carbon dioxide. *Skill (b)*

(c) Explain why the oxygen produced is drawn into the capillary tube for measuring. *Skill (b)*

(d) At which measurement position would the light intensity be greatest? *Skill (e)*

(e) What happens to the light intensity when the light is moved from the 5 cm position to the 10 cm position? *Skill (e)*

(f) When the lamp is at the 5 cm position, what other factor might change and how could this change be prevented? *Skills (b) and (g)*

(g) On a grid like Figure 5.35 draw a graph to show the results in the table. *Skill (d)*

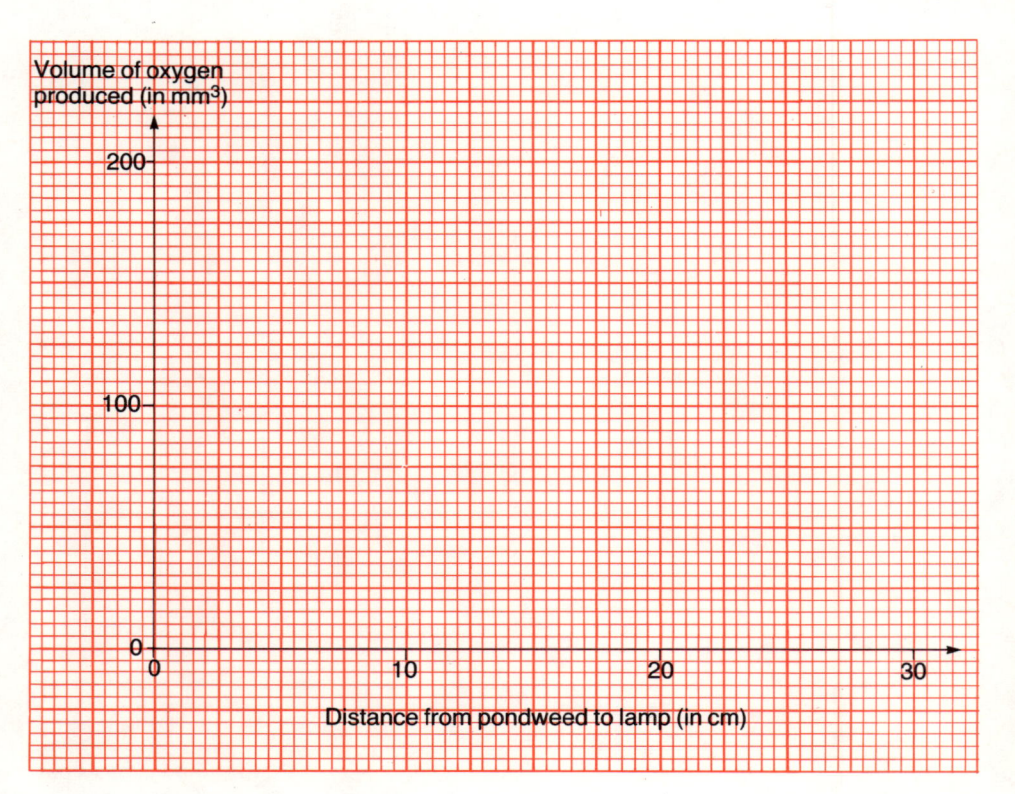

Fig. 5.35 The grid

(Graph grid: y-axis "Volume of oxygen produced (in mm³)" marked at 100 and 200; x-axis "Distance from pondweed to lamp (in cm)" marked at 0, 10, 20, 30)

(h) Describe the relationship between oxygen production and light intensity. Explain this relationship. *Skill (e)*

⟨S⟩ ⟨B⟩ **28** Two investigations were carried out on soils.

In the first investigation three funnels were half-filled with equal amounts of dry clay, loam and sand respectively. Then 50 cm³ of water was poured into each funnel *at the same time*. The volumes of water that had drained through after 15 minutes are shown in Figure 5.36.

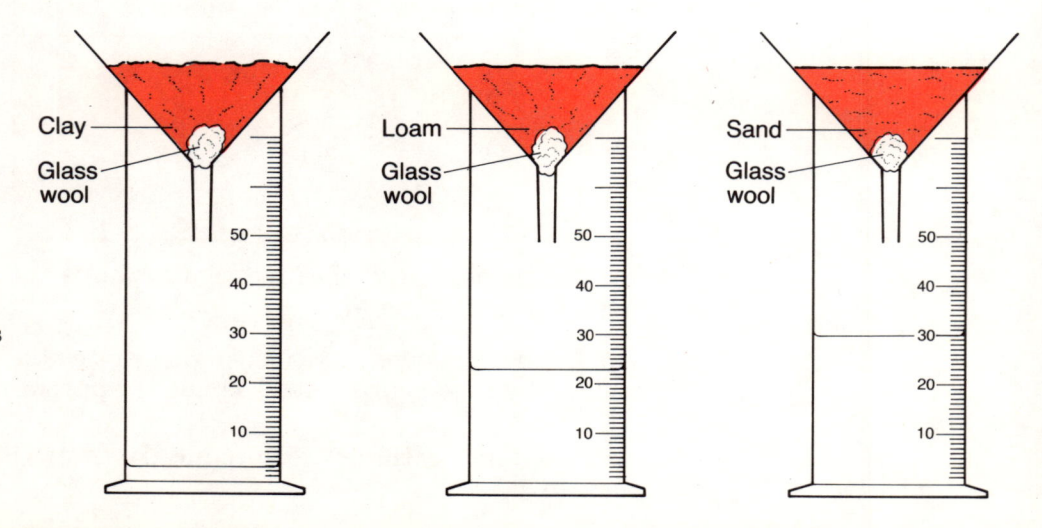

Fig. 5.36 After 15 minutes

(Three funnels with glass wool, labelled Clay, Loam, Sand, each draining into measuring cylinders marked 10–50)

48

(a) Record the volumes of water that have drained through each soil in a suitable table. *Skills (c) and (d)*

(b) Explain why all 50 cm³ of water has not drained through any of the soils. *Skill (e)*

In the second investigation three tubes (each 50 cm long) were filled with clay, loam and sand respectively (Figure 5.37). The lower end of each tube was placed in water. The levels of the water in each soil were marked on the tubes after eight hours and after three days.

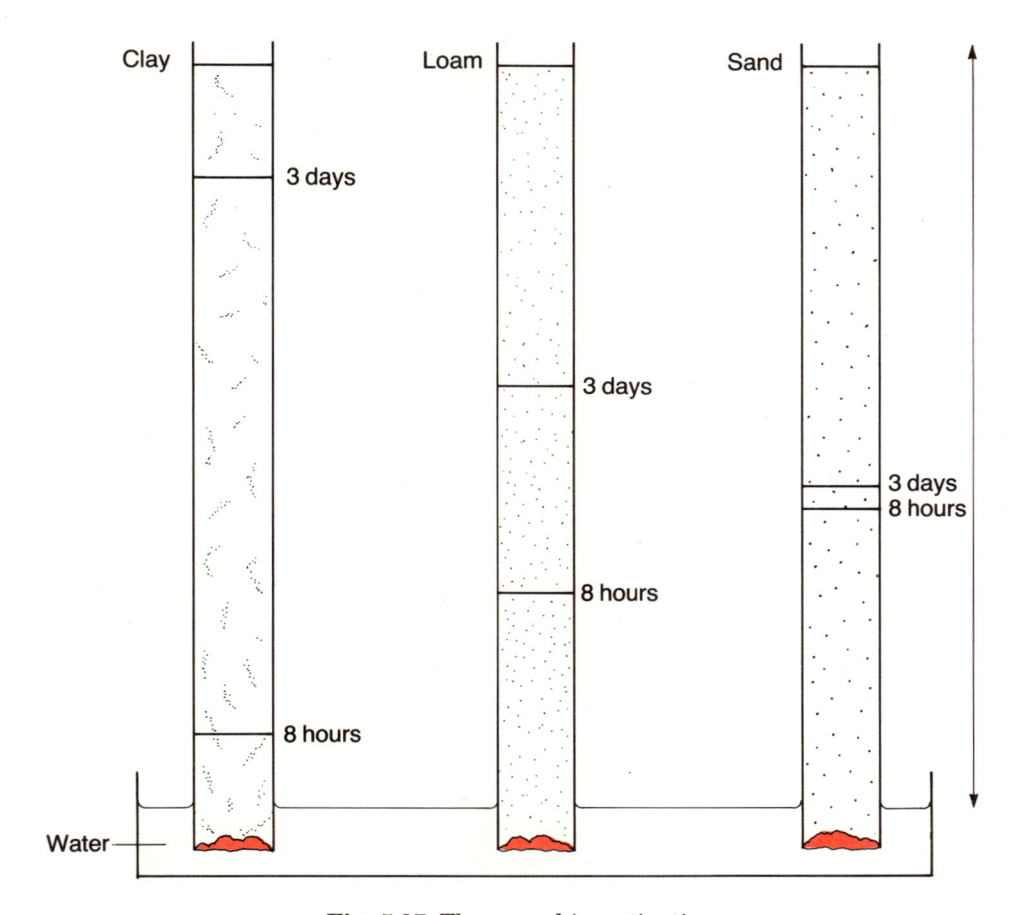

Fig. 5.37 The second investigation

(c) Work out the level of the water in each tube at these times and record your results in a suitable table. *Skills (c) and (d)*

(d) From the results of the two investigations, describe what conclusions you can draw about how well each soil *(i)* drains and *(ii)* takes up water. *Skill (e)*

29 In an investigation to study the growth of a population of yeast, some yeast was inoculated into a culture medium. A small sample of the culture was removed every hour and examined on a microscope slide ruled with squares. Figure 5.38 shows the yeast cells in one area of each of the slides.

(a) Count the number of yeast cells in each square. Record the results in a suitable table. *Skills (c) and (d)*

(b) On a grid like Figure 5.39 draw a graph of the results. *Skill (e)*

(c) Suggest why the number of yeast cells after one hour was less than the number at the start. *Skill (f)*

(d) Suggest what would happen to the yeast population if it were left in the same culture medium for several days. Explain your answer. *Skill (e)*

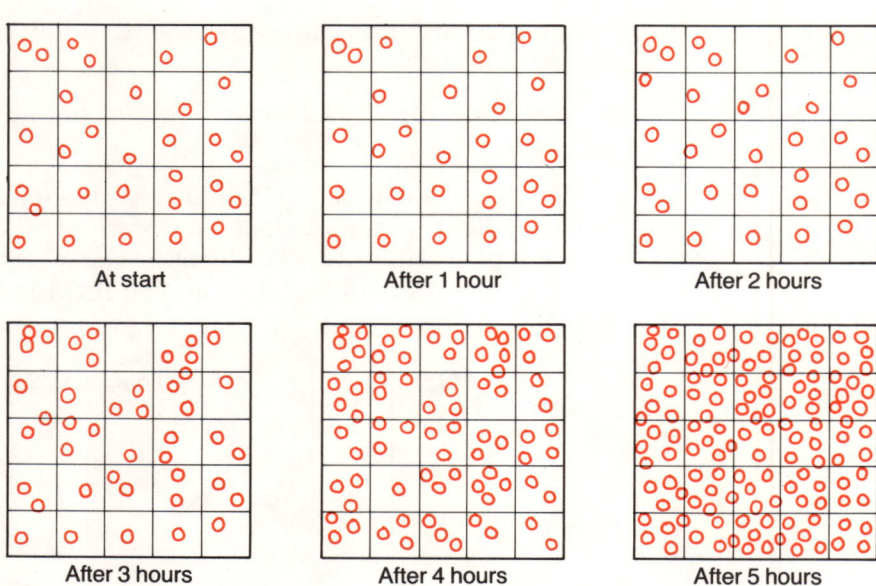

Fig. 5.38 Yeast cells

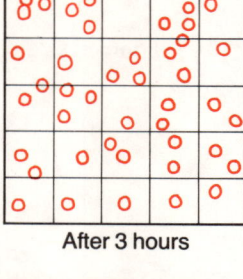

At start — After 1 hour — After 2 hours
After 3 hours — After 4 hours — After 5 hours

Fig. 5.39 The grid

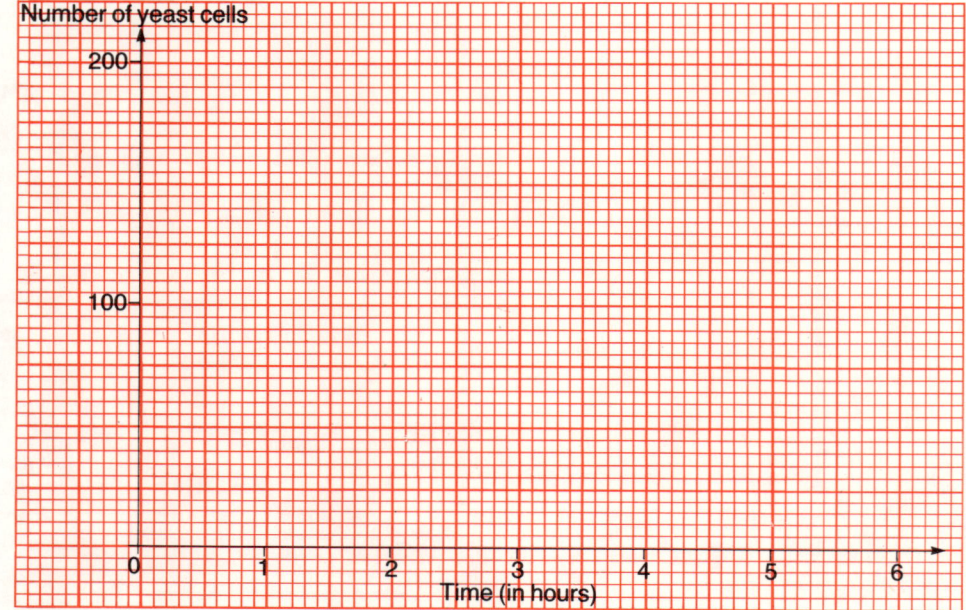

Number of yeast cells / Time (in hours)

(a) Distribution of aphids in a strong wind

(b) Distribution of aphids after wind has died down

Fig. 5.40 Distribution of aphids

⬦S⬦ ⬦B⬦

30 The drawings in Figure 5.40 show the distribution of aphids (greenfly) on the lower side of a sycamore leaf. Part (a) shows the aphids on the leaf in a strong wind. Part (b) shows them after the wind had died down.

(a) Count the number of aphids in each sector in the two drawings. Record your results in a suitable table. *Skills (c) and (d)*

(b) Describe the differences in distribution of the aphids in the two drawings. *Skill (c)*

(c) Suggest one reason in each case for:
(i) the difference in total numbers of aphids,
(ii) the difference in distribution of aphids. *Skill (e)*

⬦S⬦ ⬦P⬦

31 Test the strength of an electromagnet. When a direct electric current passes in an insulated wire wrapped around a piece of iron (Figure 5.41), the iron becomes a magnet.

Using a 4 V supply, design an experiment to show that the strength of the magnet depends upon the number of turns wrapped around the iron. You

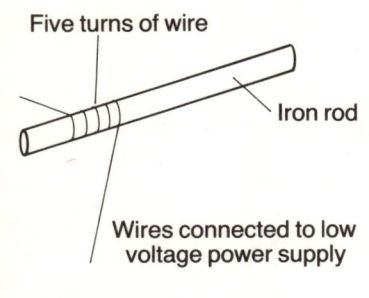

Fig. 5.41 Direct current through a wire

can use normally available laboratory apparatus. Indicate clearly the steps you would take, and how you would measure the strength of the magnet.
Skill (f)

32 When soap solution is added to rain water a lather (foam) forms immediately. Rain water is soft water.

When soap solution is added to tap water from certain sources a lather does not form immediately. Tap water like this is called hard water. A lather only forms when the hardness has been removed.

When hard water is boiled some of the hardness (called temporary hardness) is removed. The hardness which remains after boiling is called permanent hardness.

Investigation 1

Soap solution was added, a drop at a time, to 15 cm^3 of water obtained from different sources until a lather formed. The results are shown in the table below.

Water source	Number of drops of soap added to form a lather	
	before boiling	after boiling
Rain water	4	4
A	27	14
B	32	12
C	9	4
D	23	12

(a) Name a piece of apparatus suitable for adding the soap solution.
Skill (b)

(b) Which source of water was the hardest before boiling? *Skill (e)*

(c) Which source of water contained the most permanent hardness?
Skill (e)

(d) Which source of water contained the most temporary hardness?
Skill (e)

Chemicals called water softeners can be used to remove hardness and so prevent soap being wasted.

Investigation 2

This was to test the effectiveness of various substances at softening water. 1.50 g of each substance was shaken with 15 cm^3 of water from source A. The number of drops of soap solution needed to produce a lather was again found. The results are shown in the table below.

Substance added to water	Number of drops of soap solution needed to produce a lather
bath cubes	4
salt	27
Epsom salts	86
slaked lime	14

(e) Describe how the samples of substances should be accurately measured out.
Skill (b)

(f) What was the effect of Epsom salts on the *total* level of hardness?
Skill (e)

(g) What was the effect on *(i)* temporary hardness, and *(ii)* permanent hardness of each of the three other substances added? Record your answers in a table like the one below.

Substance added	Effect on temporary hardness	Effect on permanent hardness
bath cubes salt slaked lime		

Skill (e)

(h) Why was it important to use 15 cm³ of water from source A in Investigation 2 as well as in Investigation 1? *Skill (f)*

(i) The hardness of tap water is caused by certain solids dissolving in the water as it soaks through the ground. The solids can be separated from the water by converting the water to steam and then cooling the steam so that the water reforms. The solids are left behind.
Draw a labelled diagram of apparatus which could be used to produce water containing no hardness by this process, starting with 100 cm³ of tap water. *Skill (f)*

33 This is another design experiment, based upon runaway lorries. You are asked to design an experiment which compares the accelerations of two lorries released from the top of a steep hill. One of the lorries is to have twice the mass of the other. Try to base your design on experiments which you have done at school to measure and compare accelerations. Use the following design headings.
(a) Sketch of apparatus to be used.
(b) Procedure, including readings to be taken and any precautions necessary to ensure reliability.
(c) How you would draw a conclusion from your results.
Skills (e), (f) and (g)

34 Corrosion in steel central heating radiators reduces their useful life. The corrosion can be reduced by adding liquid inhibitors to the water. The following procedure was used to test the effectiveness of some inhibitors.
Step 1 Five similar pieces of steel were cleaned and degreased.
Step 2 100 cm³ of a 20 per cent solution of four different inhibitors were made up.
Step 3 Five drops of a test reagent were added to each solution. The reagent produced a blue colour in the presence of steel corrosion.
Step 4 One piece of steel was put into each of the inhibitor solutions. The fifth piece of steel was added to 100 cm³ of water with no inhibitor but containing five drops of the test reagent.
Step 5 The steel pieces were left for some months and observations made at monthly intervals.
The results are shown in the table on page 53. (The abbreviation ppt stands for precipitate.)
(a) Name pieces of apparatus suitable for:
(i) measuring out 100 cm³ of solution;
(ii) adding five drops of the test reagent. *Skill (b)*

(b) What was the purpose in this experiment of the steel in water without an inhibitor? *Skill (f)*

(c) Which inhibitor was the most effective at reducing corrosion? *Skill (e)*

(d) Put the inhibitors in order of effectiveness, putting the most effective first. *Skill (e)*

	After 1 month	After 2 months	After 3 months	After 4 months
no inhibitor	yellow ppt in water	traces of blue around steel	pale blue solution	deep blue solution
inhibitor A	faint yellow ppt	dense yellow ppt	no further change	faint blue colour in solution
inhibitor B	slight yellow ppt	dense yellow ppt	yellow ppt and sediment	no further change
inhibitor C	traces of blue around steel	pale blue throughout solution	deep blue colour in solution	no further change
inhibitor D	faint yellow ppt	dense yellow ppt	faint blue around steel	pale blue throughout solution

(e) What is surprising about the results for inhibitor C?   *Skill (e)*

(f) Describe carefully how you would investigate how effective inhibitor B is at temperatures between 20 °C and 80 °C.
You should include:
(i) enough detail for another person to carry out your procedure;
(ii) the apparatus required;
(iii) the measurements, readings or observations which should be taken.
Why would it be advisable to test the effectiveness of the inhibitors over a range of temperatures?   *Skills (b) and (f)*

(g) A radiator was found to corrode where it came into contact with a brass control valve. Devise a simple experiment to show that iron corrodes faster in contact with brass or copper but more slowly in contact with zinc.   *Skill (f)*

35 The apparatus was set up as shown in Figure 5.42. After a few days the mustard seeds in A started to germinate but the mustard seeds in B did not germinate. The steel wool in B started to rust.

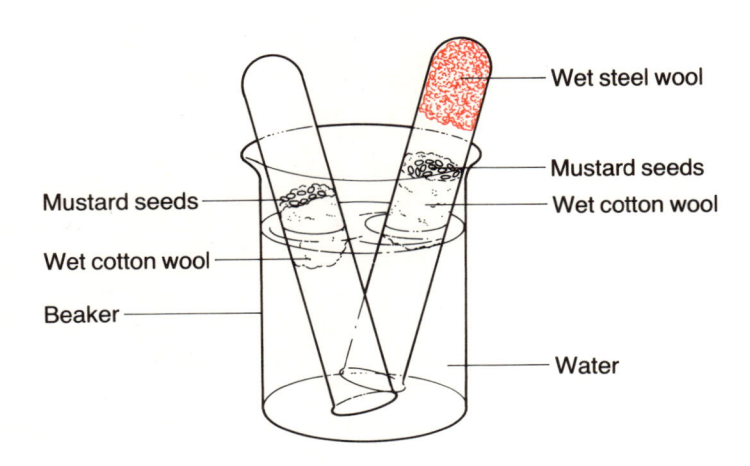

Fig. 5.42 The apparatus set up

What conclusions can you draw from this experiment?   *Skill (e)*

36 A gardener discovers a number of earwigs inside the hollow stem of a dead plant in her garden.
(a) Suggest three factors which could have acted as stimuli for the earwigs to go into the hollow stem.   *Skill (f)*

The gardener also found earwigs in the flowers of some of her prize roses. The petals were partly eaten. She wondered whether the earwigs found the roses by scent or their colour.

(b) Design an investigation to find out whether either of these suggestions is true. *Skill (f)*

◆S◆ ◆B◆ **37** Catalase is an enzyme found in actively metabolizing tissues such as those of the liver, kidney and germinating seeds. It removes a common toxic end product of metabolism – hydrogen peroxide. As hydrogen peroxide builds up inside cells it becomes extremely harmful so it has to be removed very quickly. The reaction catalysed by catalase is:

hydrogen peroxide → water + oxygen
$$2 H_2O_2 (aq) \rightarrow 2 H_2O(l) + O_2(g)$$

The rate of reaction can be measured by collecting the oxygen gas that is produced.

(a) Using the apparatus in Figure 5.43, draw a diagram to show how you would collect and measure the volume of oxygen produced when five germinating peas are added to 10 cm³ of hydrogen peroxide solution. *Skills (b) and (f)*

(b) Suggest a suitable control to show that the germinating peas are the source of the enzyme catalase. *Skill (b)*

(c) Why is a graduated syringe barrel used? *Skill (b)*

(d) How would you carry out the experiment to show how the rate of reaction changes over a period of five minutes? *Skill (f)*

(e) How would you modify the experiment to investigate the effects of *(i)* temperature and *(ii)* pH on this enzyme catalysed reaction? *Skill (g)*

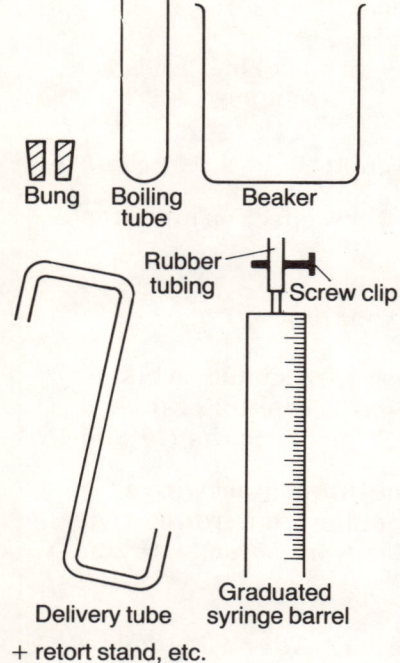

Fig. 5.43 The apparatus

◆S◆ ◆B◆ ◆C◆ **38** The Benedict's test is used to show that reducing sugars such as glucose are dissolved in a solution. An experiment was carried out to find the lowest concentration of glucose which can be detected by this test. A report of the experiment is given below.

> *(1)* 10 g of glucose was dissolved and made up to a volume of 1 dm³. This solution was labelled A.
>
> *(2)* 10 cm³ of solution A was diluted until it had a volume of 100 cm³. This solution was labelled B.
>
> *(3)* 10 cm³ of solution B was diluted to 100 cm³. This solution was labelled C.
>
> *(4)* 10 cm³ of solution C was diluted to 100 cm³. This solution was labelled D.
>
> *(5)* 5 cm³ of each solution was put into separate labelled test tubes.
>
> *(6)* 10 drops of Benedict's solution was placed in each test tube. The test tubes were placed in the same boiling water bath.
>
> *(7)* The test tubes were watched for the first appearance of a green cloudiness in the solution.

The results are shown in the table below.

Test tube	Glucose solution	Time for cloudiness (in s)
1	A	50
2	B	85
3	C	195
4	D	no cloudiness after 600 s

(a) Which of the pipettes in Figure 5.44 is correctly filled to deliver exactly 10 cm³ of sugar solution? *Skill (b)*

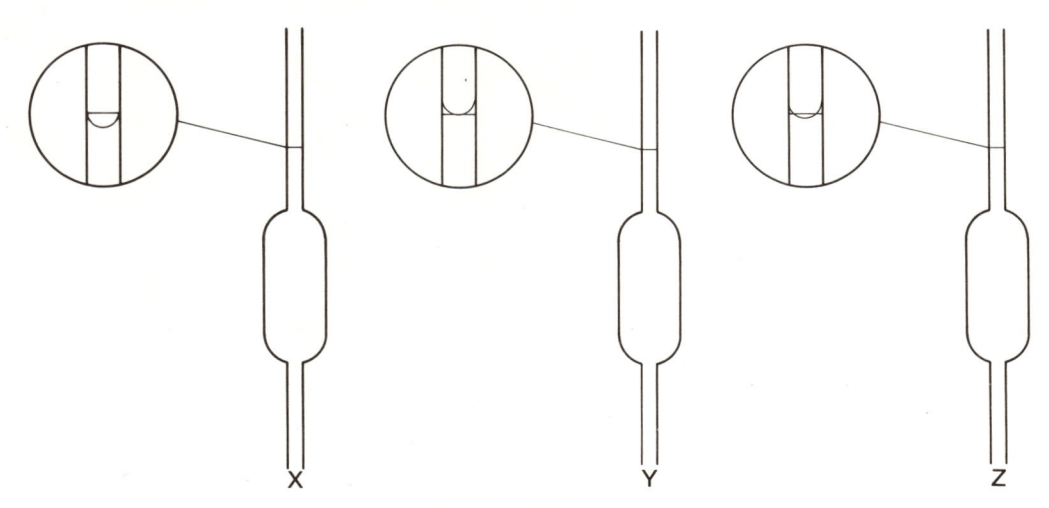

Fig. 5.44 Which one?

Benedict's solution is used to test for reducing agents such as glucose. Fehling's solutions can be used as an alternative.

(b) Solution A has a glucose concentration of 10 g per dm³. What are the concentrations of glucose in B, C and D? *Skill (a)*

(c) Describe carefully the steps that should be taken to prepare solution B from solution A. *Skills (a) and (b)*

(d) Why were the test tubes placed in the same boiling water bath? *Skill (a)*

(e) What piece of apparatus is most suitable for:
(i) measuring out 5 cm³ of glucose solution into the test tubes;
(ii) adding the Benedict's solution to the test tubes? *Skill (b)*

(f) What is the lowest concentration of glucose detected by the Benedict's solution? *Skill (e)*

(g) How could the experiment be extended to find out if Benedict's solution will detect even lower concentrations than the one given in (**f**)? *Skill (g)*

(h) Give two safety precautions which should be taken in this experiment. *Skill (b)*

(i) Glucose will diffuse through dialysis (Visking) tubing. Using the information in this question, devise an experiment to test the hypothesis that temperature increases the rate of diffusion through the tubing. *Skill (f)*

(j) Potassium manganate(VII) is a dark purple crystalline solid. It dissolves in water to give a purple or pink-coloured solution. Devise an experiment to find the lowest concentration of potassium manganate(VII) which will produce a coloured solution.
What does this experiment tell you about the size of the particles present in potassium manganate(VII)? *Skills (e) and (f)*

Ⓢ Ⓑ Ⓒ **39** Some investigations were carried out to compare two potting composts which contain sand, grit, peat, water, inorganic fertilizer and air.

Investigation 1

1000 g of each compost were placed in an oven at 105 °C for several hours. The mass of each compost was found at the end of each hour. The results are shown in the table on page 56.

(a) Name the substance lost from the compost during the heating which caused the loss of mass. *Skill (e)*

Time (in hours)	Mass of compost A (in g)	Mass of compost B (in g)
0	1000	1000
1	970	975
2	890	895
3	845	855
4	820	830
5	810	815
6	800	805
7	800	805

(b) What type of balance would be most suitable for this investigation? *Skill (b)*

(c) Why were no further measurements of mass made after seven hours? *Skill (e)*

(d) What was the mass loss from compost A after seven hours? *Skill (e)*

(e) What percentage of the mass of compost A was lost in seven hours? *Skill (e)*

(f) Both composts lost more mass in the second hour than in the first hour. Explain this. *Skill (b)*

(g) When the investigation was repeated with composts maintained at 300 °C the total mass loss was greater than at 105 °C. What other substance, present in the compost, was removed by heating at the higher temperature? *Skill (e)*

Investigation 2

Compost A	Compost B
Experiment 1 When 100 cm^3 of water was added to 100 cm^3 of compost the resulting mixture had a volume of 150 cm^3	*Experiment 2* When 100 cm^3 of water was added to 100 cm^3 of compost the resulting mixture had a volume of 165 cm^3
Experiment 3 100 cm^3 of water was poured onto 200 cm^3 of compost. In 15 minutes 100 cm^3 of water had soaked through	*Experiment 4* 100 cm^3 of water was poured onto 200 cm^3 of compost. In 15 minutes 50 cm^3 of water had soaked through
Experiment 5 The pH of the compost was 6	*Experiment 6* The pH of the compost was 8

(h) Name a piece of apparatus suitable for measuring the water in Experiments 1 and 2. *Skill (b)*

(i) What conclusion can be drawn about the properties of Compost A compared with Compost B from Experiments 3 and 4? *Skill (e)*

(j) What information do the pH values obtained in Experiments 5 and 6 give? *Skill (e)*

(k) The table below shows the type of soil on which certain plants grow best.

Soil	Type	Plant
acidic	well-drained	blueberries
acidic	water-retaining	azalea
neutral	well-drained	gooseberries
neutral	water-retaining	pineapple
alkaline	well-drained	geranium
alkaline	water-retaining	cabbage

Which plant in the table is best planted in Compost A? *Skill (e)*

40 Figure 5.45 shows how to carry out an experiment to test a leaf for the presence of starch.

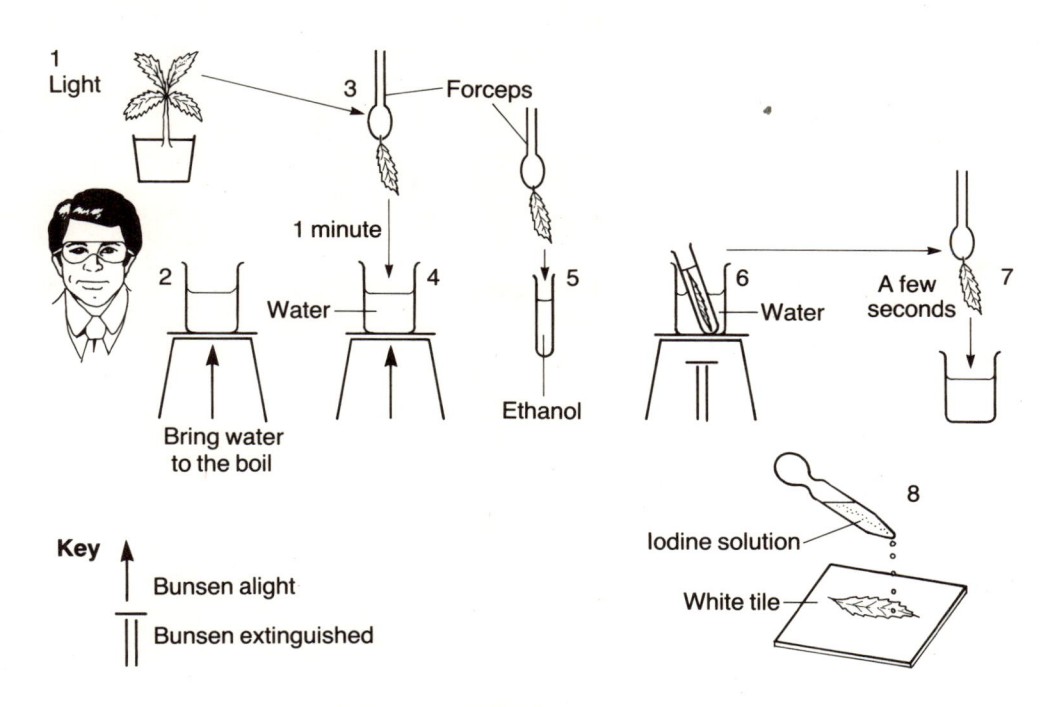

Fig. 5.45 Testing a leaf for starch

(a) What major safety precaution is being taken in the experiment? *Skill (b)*

(b) What was the ethanol used for? *Skill (a)*

(c) Why was the leaf dipped into water in 4? *Skill (a)*

(d) Rewrite the instructions given in Figure 5.45 as a set of written instructions. Make sure that all safety precautions are stressed. *Skill (a)*

(e) Devise an experiment to show that leaves need light for photosynthesis. *Skill (f)*

41 The apparatus in Figure 5.46 was used to compare the heat produced by three different liquid fuels.

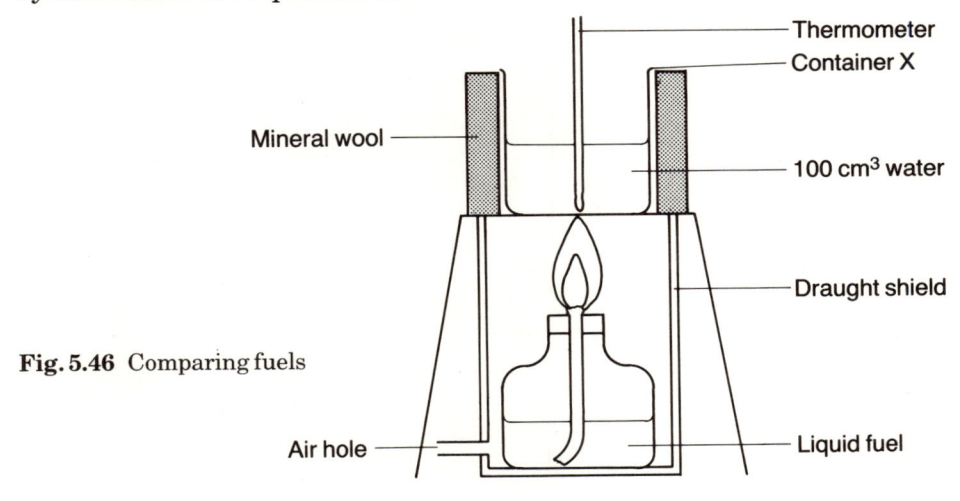

Fig. 5.46 Comparing fuels

100 cm^3 of water was placed in the container labelled X. Mineral wool was wrapped around this container. The temperature was recorded (Figure 5.47(a)). The mass of the burner and its fuel was found. The burner was placed inside the draught shield and the wick was lit.

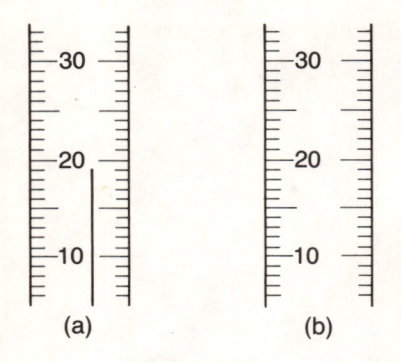

Fig. 5.47
(a) the reading
(b) mark the mercury level

The water was stirred continuously and the temperature allowed to rise by 9 °C. The flame was extinguished and the mass of the burner was again found. The procedure was repeated with the other two fuels.
The results are shown in the following table.

	Fuel A	Fuel B	Fuel C
mass of burner at start	14.03 g	13.02 g	13.43 g
mass of burner at end	13.32 g	12.44 g	12.78 g

(a) What is the most suitable substance for making the container X? Explain your choice. *Skill (b)*

(b) What is the purpose of the mineral wool? *Skill (a)*

(c) Why is it important to have a draught shield? *Skill (a)*

(d) What mass of water was used in each experiment? *Skill (a)*

(e) What is the temperature shown on the thermometer in Figure 5.47(a)? *Skill (c)*

(f) Figure 5.47(b) shows the thermometer at the end of one of the experiments. Mark on this thermometer the position of the mercury.
Skill (c)

(g) Which of the fuels, A, B or C, produces the most heat per gram of fuel? Explain how you decided. *Skill (e)*

(h) Calculate the amount of heat gained by the water in each case. (Specific heat capacity of water is 4.2 J per g per °C.) *Skill (e)*

(i) Explain why, for the purpose of this investigation, the heat losses to the apparatus and the air can be ignored. *Skill (f)*

(j) Suggest any improvements that could be made to the experiment which would give results closer to the results given in a data book. *Skill (g)*

(k) In practice, it is more useful to find which fuel produces most heat per cubic centimetre. Outline a method you would use to make this comparison. Include:
(i) any apparatus you would need;
(ii) any readings you would make;
(iii) a table of results in which you could record your results;
(iv) how you would interpret your results. *Skills (b), (c), (d) and (e)*

S P 42 An investigation was carried out to find the mass needed to raise a ruler. The apparatus was set up as in Figure 5.48. The ruler was fastened to the edge of the bench using adhesive tape as a hinge.

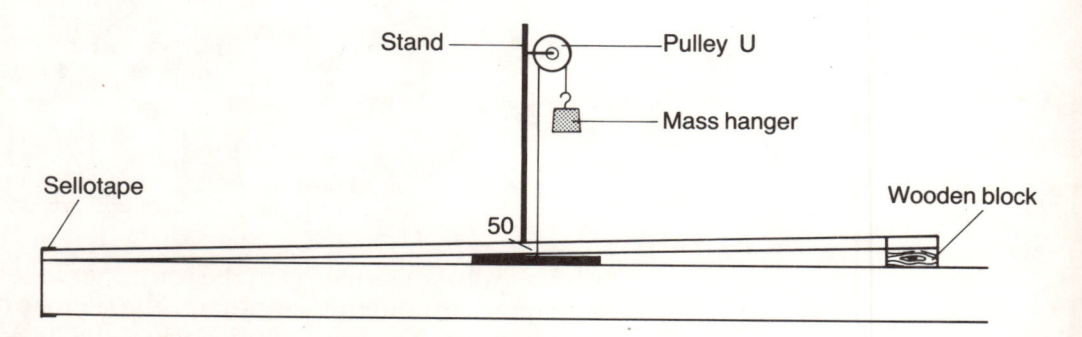

Fig. 5.48 The apparatus

The string was looped around the ruler at the 50 cm mark. The mass needed *just* to lift the 100 cm end of the ruler off the wooden block was 120 g.

The mass of the hanger was changed to 110 g. The position of the string loop was changed until it was positioned for 110 g *just* to lift the 100 cm end of the ruler off the wooden block.

The experiment was repeated with 100 g, 90 g, 80 g and 70 g masses. All the results are recorded in the table below.

Position of string loop	Mass needed to raise ruler (in g)
50 cm mark	120
54 cm mark	110
60 cm mark	100
67 cm mark	90
75 cm mark	80
86 cm mark	70

(a) Why was it necessary to raise the end of the ruler on a wooden block?
Skill (b)

(b) Plot a graph of the results on a grid like Figure 5.49. Plot distance from the hinge on the *x*-axis and mass required to lift the ruler on the *y*-axis.
Skill (d)

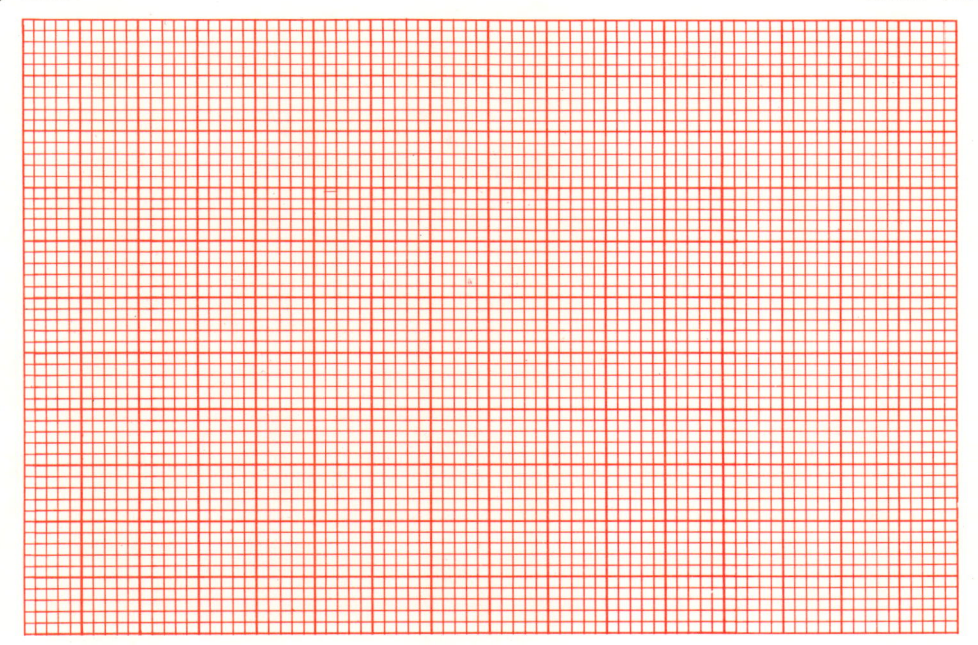

Fig. 5.49

(c) What mass would have *just* lifted the ruler when the loop is placed:
(i) 70 cm from the hinge;
(ii) 57 cm from the hinge?
Skill (e)

(d) What can you conclude about the relationship between the mass required *just* to lift the ruler, and the distance the loop is from the hinge?
Skill (e)

43 Carry out an experiment to investigate the 'effect of light' on the resistance of a light dependent resistor (LDR).

A light dependent resistor was carefully covered with a cap of black paper. A circuit was set up, as in Figure 5.50, to measure the current flowing through the LDR and the potential difference across it.

Fig. 5.50 The circuit

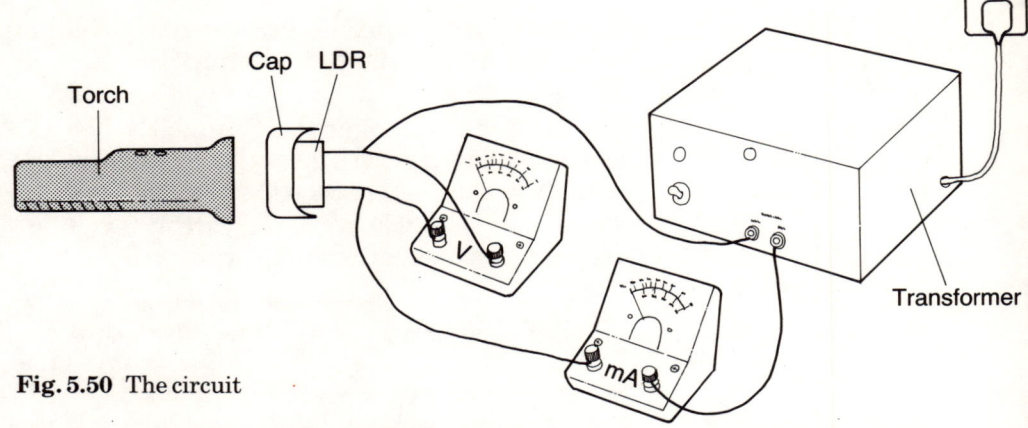

The torch was set at a fixed distance (10 cm) from the LDR. One pin-hole was made in the cap and the potential difference adjusted to read 4 V. The current reading was taken.

A second pin-hole of equal size was made in the cap to double the light hitting the LDR. The potential difference was adjusted to read 4 V and a current reading was made. The process of adding pin-holes and taking readings of the potential difference and current was continued until there were six pin-holes.

The resistance of the LDR can be calculated by dividing the potential difference (V) by the current (I).

$$\frac{V}{I} = R$$

The results are shown in the table below.

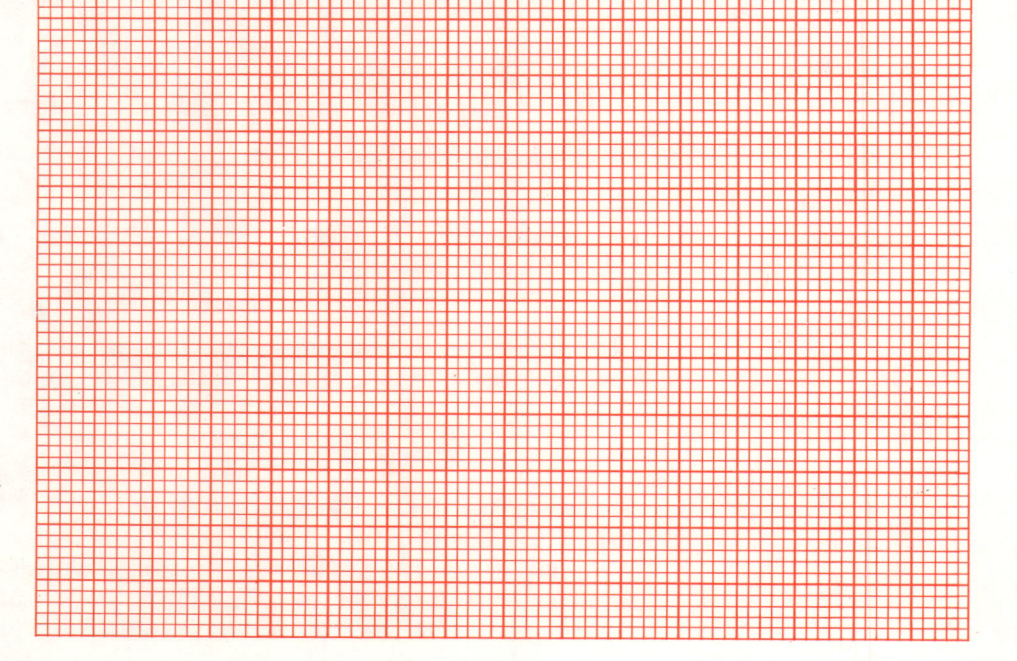

Number of holes	Potential difference (in V)	Current (in mA)	Current (in A)	Resistance (in Ω)
1	4	1.7	0.0017	2353
2	4	2.4		
3	4	2.8		
4	4	3.2		
5	4	3.5		
6	4	3.7		

Fig. 5.51

(a) Which of the meters, voltmeter or milliammeter, is connected in parallel with the LDR? *Skill (b)*

(b) Why is it essential to make all of the pin-holes of equal size? *Skill (b)*

(c) Complete the table by converting the current to amps and calculating the resistance for each reading. *Skill (d)*

(d) On a grid like Figure 5.51, plot a graph of 'the number of holes' against resistance. *Skill (d)*

(e) How does the resistance of the LDR change as the light level is increased? *Skill (e)*

44 The pH of a solution can be found using a pH meter. Before use, the electrode is dipped into a solution of known pH.

(a) Why is the electrode dipped into the solution of known pH? *Skill (b)*

(b) Why is a pH meter more suitable than Universal indicator for finding the pH of a solution of blackcurrant cordial? *Skill (b)*

(c) The table below shows some indicators and the colours they are at the pH given.

pH	1	2	3	4	5	6	7	8	9	10	11	12
methyl orange	red →				←	yellow						
crystal violet	green →	← blue →				← violet						
thymolphthalein	colourless								→ ←	blue		
rosolic acid	yellow					→			←	red		

The pH values of some solutions are given below.

nitric acid   pH 1
citric acid   pH 5
aqueous ammonia   pH 10
calcium hydroxide   pH 12

(i) In a table like the one below, write the colour seen when the indicators are added to the solutions named.

Indicator	Solution	Colour seen
methyl orange	aqueous ammonia	
crystal violet	nitric acid	
thymolphthalein	citric acid	
rosolic acid	calcium hydroxide	

Skills (a) and (e)

(ii) Which indicator gives the same colour with both citric acid and calcium hydroxide? *Skill (f)*

(iii) At which pH value would rosolic acid be orange? *Skill (e)*

45 The following table shows sets of results obtained when sodium hydroxide solution and ammonia solution were added to solutions of salts. Use these tables to answer the questions which follow.

Addition of sodium hydroxide solution

Name of solution	Colour of solution	Change on adding 5 drops of sodium hydroxide solution	Further change on adding excess
copper(II) sulphate	blue	light blue ppt formed	no further change
zinc sulphate	colourless	white ppt formed	ppt redissolves
potassium chloride	colourless	no ppt	no ppt
lead(II) nitrate	colourless	white ppt formed	ppt redissolves
iron(II) sulphate	pale green	dark green ppt formed	no further change
iron(III) sulphate	orange/yellow	orange/brown ppt formed	no further change
aluminium sulphate	colourless	white ppt formed	ppt redissolves

Addition of ammonia solution

copper(II) sulphate	blue	light blue ppt formed	royal blue solution formed when ppt redissolves

(a) Which of the hydroxides formed in this experiment are soluble in water? *Skill (e)*

(b) Which of the hydroxides will redissolve in excess sodium hydroxide solution? *Skill (e)*

(c) Using the information in the tables, explain how you would distinguish between iron(II) ions and iron(III) ions. *Skill (f)*

(d) You have two unlabelled bottles containing colourless solutions. One bottle contains sodium hydroxide solution and the other contains ammonia solution. Using the information in the tables, devise a simple experiment to show how you would find out which of these solutions is which. *Skill (f)*

SECTION SIX

Answers to questions

1(a) A Lesser black-backed gull
  B Little gull
  C Herring gull

(b) Kittiwake

(c) No information on colour of back, so the same feature might apply to any birds after this point in the key. It is essential to work through a key.

(d) Make model birds with bills, some without red spots and others with red spots. Present the models to your chicks several times and count the number of pecks.

2(a)

Stonefly nymph	Mayfly nymph
Long antennae	Short antennae
Large body	Small body
Projecting mouthparts	No mouthparts visible
Large head	Small head
Distinct neck	No neck
3 visible segments in thorax	Only 2 segments of thorax visible
Wing outgrowth on 2 segments	Only 1 pair of wing outgrowths
Gills on thorax	Gills on abdomen
Pair of claws on each leg	Single claw on each leg
No hairs on first part of first leg	Hairs all along first leg
2 cerci	3 cerci
Hairless cerci	Hairy cerci
10 abdominal segments	8 abdominal segments

(You are only expected to find any *nine* of these to make up the ten required.)

(b) Stonefly 42 mm
  Mayfly 15 mm

(Allow yourself an error of +1 mm or −1 mm for the mayfly and +2 mm or −2 mm for the stonefly. Do not forget the units.)

(c) Flattened body to reduce resistance.
  Claws to hold onto the stones.
  Gills to get oxygen from the water.

3(a) Your circuit diagram should show the ammeter in series with the heater and the voltmeter in parallel with it. One possible way of showing this is given in Figure 6.1.

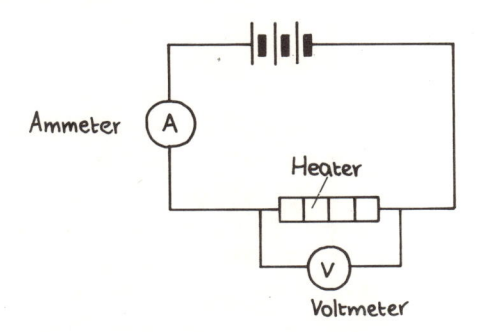

Fig. 6.1

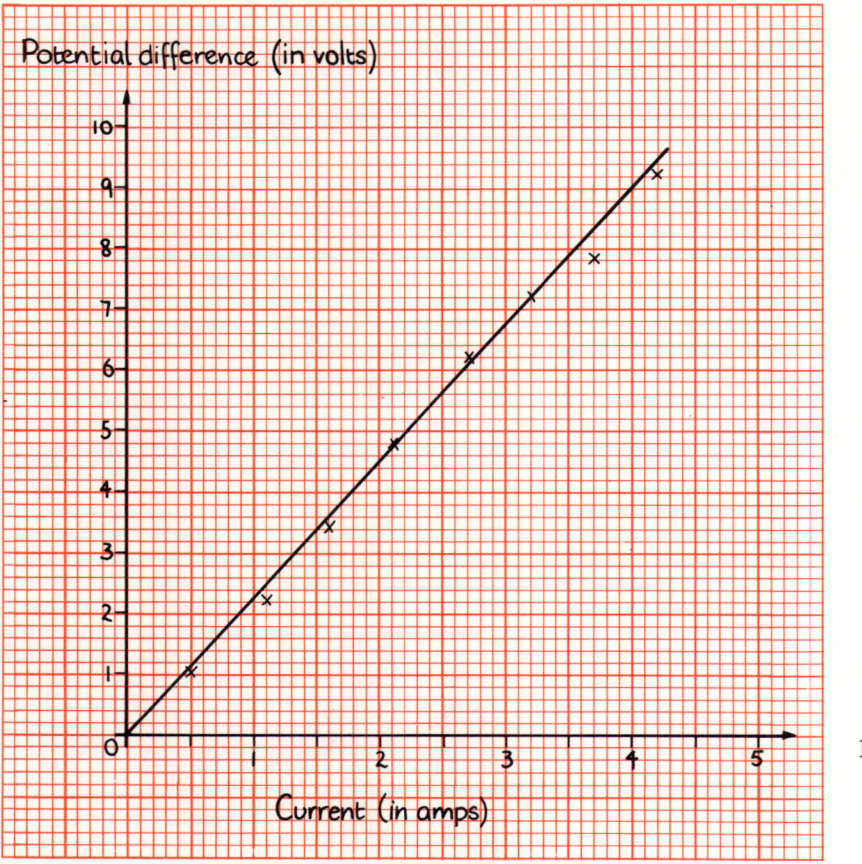

Fig. 6.2

(b) Make sure you understand the graph scale before you start plotting. Figure 6.2 shows the graph you should have obtained drawing the best straight line through the points.

(c) The resistance values (rounded to one decimal place) are, from the top, 2.0 Ω, 2.1 Ω, 2.2 Ω, 2.2 Ω, 2.3 Ω, 2.2 Ω, 2.1 Ω, 2.2 Ω.

(d) Taking into account the limits of the precision of the experiment, the best conclusion to reach is that the resistance stays the same as the current increases.

Not all of the points lie on the straight line because of slight errors in the experiment.

The gradient of the graph is a good indicator of the resistance. If the slope is increasing then so is the resistance. In this case the constant slope indicates that the resistance is not changing.

4(a)

Temperature (in °C)	Current (in A)
10	0.10
20	0.16
36	0.25
58	0.43
83	0.81
100	0.97

(b)

Resistance (in Ω)	Temperature (in °C)
90	10
56	20
36	36
21	58
11	83
9	100

You should have arranged them in ascending order. Not all of the readings were easy to make.

(c) Figure 6.3 shows the graph you should have obtained. You should have drawn the best smooth curve possible through the points and not joined them up with straight lines.

(d) As the temperature increases, the resistance decreases.

(e) Draw a line across from 45 Ω on the resistance axis. Then draw down to the temperature axis.

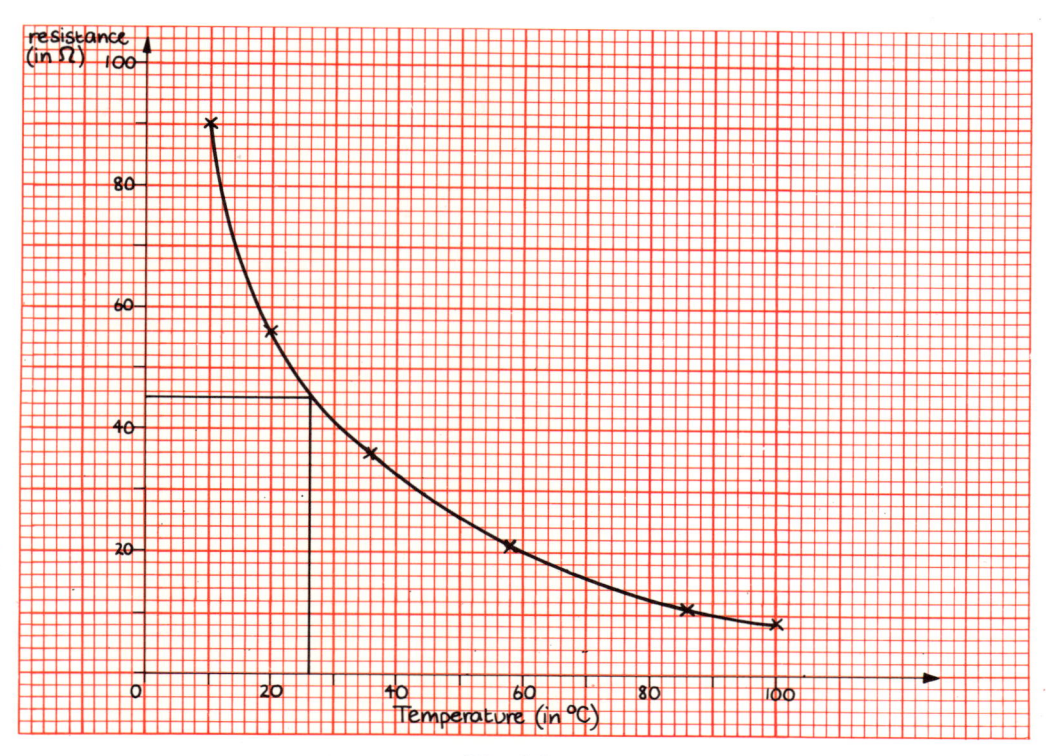

Fig. 6.3

Your result might be slightly different (27 – 29 °C), depending upon how you drew your curve.

5(a) Substance A is probably sulphate of ammonia. Substance B is probably garden lime.

(b) On the basis of this evidence I believe that Joe Bloggs is guilty. However, it would be necessary to carry out further tests on A and B to find out their exact composition.

6 There are different diagrams that you could draw. However, you should have:

(a) a supply of carbon dioxide;

(b) the carbon dioxide being converted to carbon monoxide by passing the gas over red hot charcoal;

(c) the gas bubbling through potassium hydroxide solution to dissolve the carbon dioxide;

(d) the carbon monoxide being collected over water.

Figure 6.4 shows a suitable labelled diagram

Fig. 6.4

7(a) A graduated pipette, burette or small syringe.

(b) Put them in a water bath or large beaker of water at 25 °C.

(c) As a control. To see whether the enzymes produced a faster reaction than water alone.
(d) Enzyme 2.
(e) *(i)* The graph is shown in Figure 6.5.

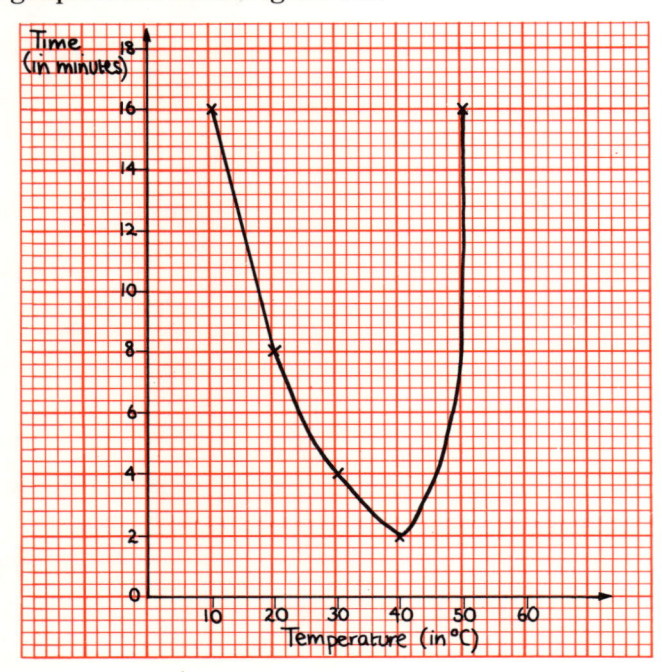

Fig. 6.5

(ii) The higher the temperature the faster the rate of reaction is, up to a maximum of 40 °C. Beyond this the rate of reaction falls. Up to 40 °C the rate of reaction approximately doubles every ten degree temperature rise.

(f) Measure 10 cm^3 of 1 per cent starch solution into, say, five test tubes. Add 1 cm^3 of enzyme 2 and 4 cm^3 of water to the first tube. To the second test tube add 2 cm^3 of enzyme 2 and 3 cm^3 of water. Continue until the fifth test tube contains 5 cm^3 of enzyme 2 and no water.

Put all of the test tubes in a water bath at 25 °C and test for starch at two-minute intervals. If the hypothesis is correct starch should be used up the more quickly the more concentrated the enzyme solution is in the starch.

(g) Figure 6.6 shows two ways of carrying out this experiment.

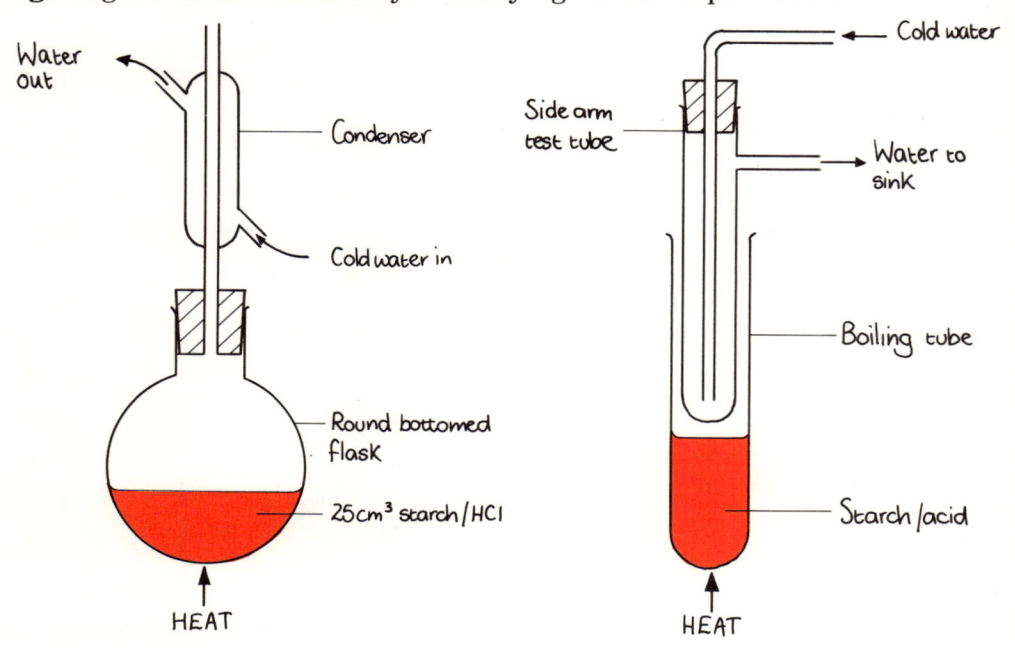

Fig. 6.6

8 Figure 6.7 shows one student's answer to this question.

> *Figure 6.7 shows typical freehand sketches that you might have to make. Draw these in pencil and label important features in ink.*

> Wrap some cloth round each of two beakers and wet the cloth round one of them. Pour some hot water from the kettle into the beakers and put a thermometer into each.
>
> beaker covered with dry cloth   beaker covered with wet cloth
>
> After a few minutes see which thermometer shows the higher reading. Its beaker has the better insulation.

Fig. 6.7 A student's answer

Whilst this method might give the student an answer to the problem, and perhaps two out of six marks, it is totally unreliable. Before reading on, try to list the areas of unreliability in the experiment, then see how many of these are overcome by the next student, in Figure 6.8.

This is a much better attempt at answering the question and worthy of six out of six. The student has thought about some of the problems involved and produced some sensible ways of overcoming them.

> Take one of the containers and wrap some cloth round it. It does not matter which container, so long as I use the same one for both experiments, then I know that my experiment is concerned with comparing wet and dry clothing rather than shiny and dull containers.
>
> Measure out a fixed amount, say 250 cm³, of hot water using a measuring cylinder.
>
> Taking care with the hot water, pour it into the beaker and put a lid on top (to prevent convection currents). Take the thermometer reading and start the clock. Take the thermometer reading each minute and write the results in a table. Stop the experiment after there has been a significant temperature drop.
>
> Now wet the cloth and repeat the experiment. To find which is the better insulator I would compare the times taken to cool between the

continued

continued

same two temperatures, not just the same temperature difference. This is because the rate at which something cools depends on the temperature it is at.

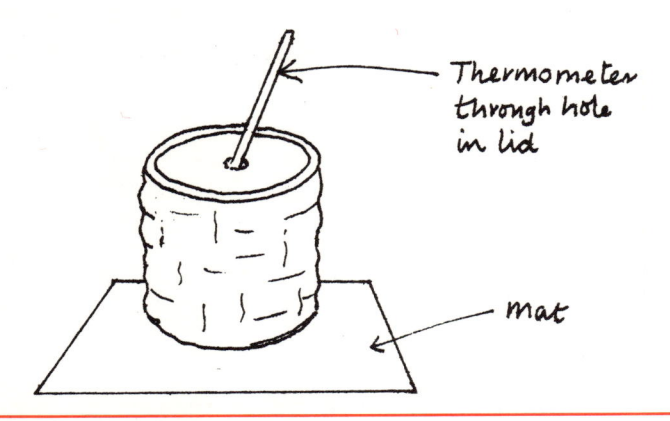

Fig. 6.8 A better answer

9(a) No gas will be collected in the gas syringe until corks are put into the two arms of the U-tube.

(b) Powder packs too closely – not allowing the gas to pass through it.

(c) Ammonia dissolves in the water produced during the reaction.

(d) There are different approaches to this type of problem. Here are two alternatives.

Method 1

Solid fertilizers added to water, stirred and 'timed' to see which disappears more rapidly. Crystals of fertilizer should be the same size. The volume of water used should be the same in both experiments.

The temperature of the water should be the same in both.

Same mass of each fertilizer used in both. The mixtures should be stirred in the same way.

Method 2

Stir the mixtures of fertilizer and water for fixed times. Filter off any fertilizer which has not dissolved. Evaporate each solution to find the mass of fertilizer left after the water has boiled away. Other variables controlled as before. The evaporating basin with the most fertilizer left after evaporation contains the more soluble fertilizer.

Either of these methods would be suitable.

10(a)

Potato cylinder	Original length (in mm)	Final length (in mm)	Change in length (in mm)
1	50	55	5
2	50	50	0
3	50	46	4

(b) Cylinder 1 – Water diffuses into the potato cells by osmosis. The cells expand and cause the cylinder to increase in length.

Cylinder 3 – Water diffuses out of the potato cells by osmosis. The cells decrease in size and the cylinder decreases in length.

(c) The concentration will have decreased. Water leaving the potato cells will dilute the sugar solution.

(d) The concentration of the cell contents is the same as that of the surrounding solution.

(e) Investigate change in mass of the potato cylinders. Measure the initial mass and then reweigh after 24 hours. This shows the mass of water which enters or leaves the cylinders.

11(a) The scale readings are, from the top, 30.9 cm, 31.8 cm, 32.7 cm, 33.8 cm, 36.2 cm.

Subtracting the initial length gives extensions of 0.9 cm, 1.8 cm, 2.7 cm, 3.8 cm and 6.2 cm.

(b) Figure 6.9 shows the graph that you should have plotted.

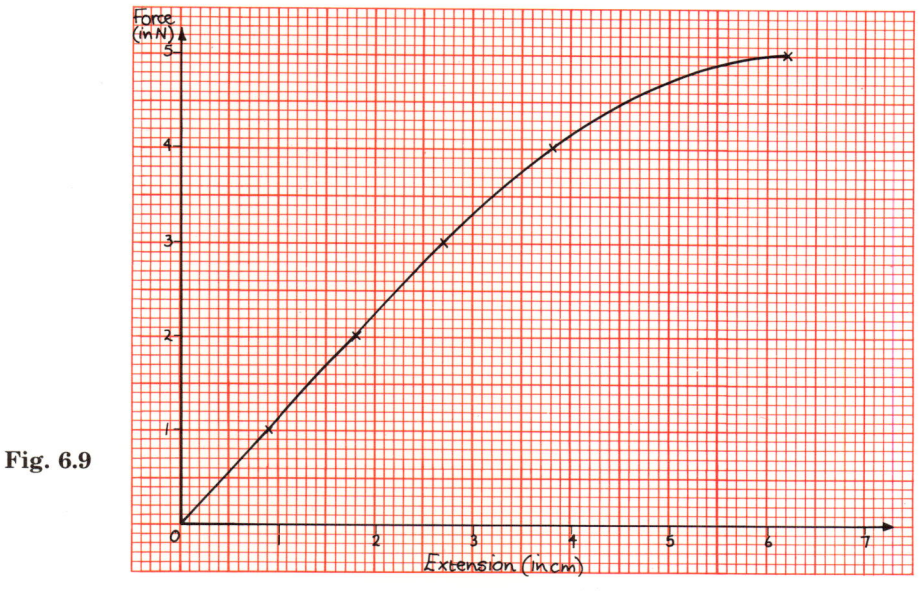

Fig. 6.9

(c) The extensions go up in equal-sized steps at first but then these steps get bigger. This is shown clearly on the graph.

(d) To find the precise breaking point, Sarah needs to increase the force in units smaller than 1 N. There are several possibilities. She could use a can of sand for the load. The amount of sand could be increased slowly until the nylon line broke. Then the can of sand could be weighed.

12(a) Crush up the mineral. Heat the mixture.

(b) No more carbon dioxide gas produced.

(c) Filter/decant/centifuge. Wash the residue with distilled water. Add the washings to the solution.

(d) Ammeter, variable resistance, balance.

(e) Mass of copper cathode before electrolysis. Mass of copper cathode after electrolysis. Difference in mass is the mass of copper deposited.

(f) The solution would become colourless. Continue to pass a current until the cathode achieves a constant mass.

(g)(i) 2.95 g (ii) 2.0 g (iii) 5%
(iv) Experimental error. Variation in the copper content of different samples of the mineral.

13(a) Figure 6.10 shows apparatus suitable for the experiment. The reaction can be started by releasing the thread so that the test tube falls and the magnesium and acid come into contact.

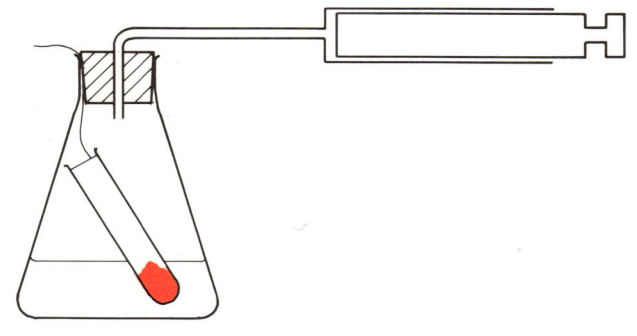

Fig. 6.10

(b) *(i)* The graphs are shown in Figure 6.11. *(ii)* 50 cm^3

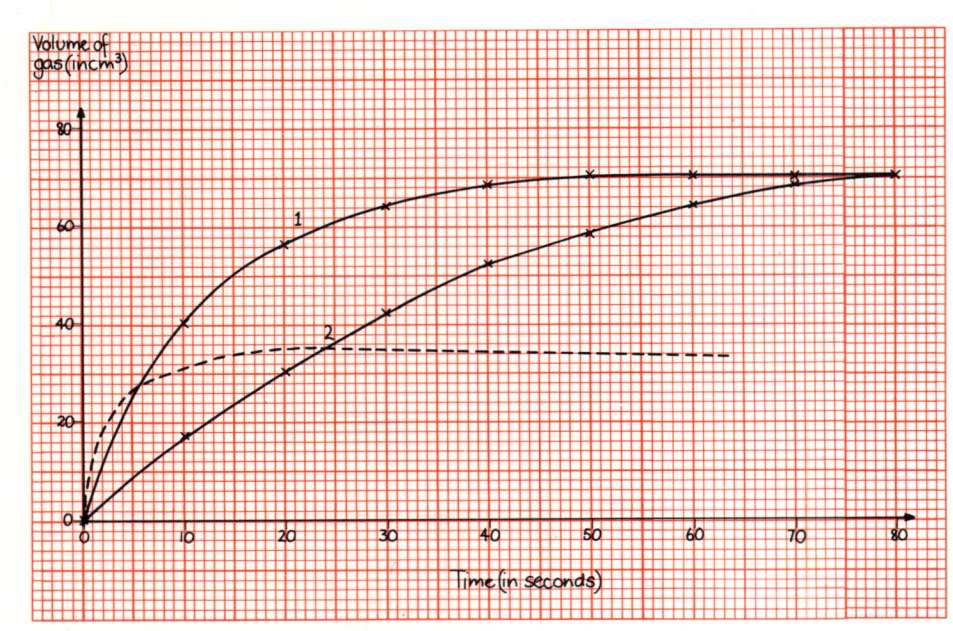

Fig. 6.11

(c) *(i)* Measure two equal lengths of magnesium ribbon. This assumes that the magnesium ribbon is of uniform cross section.

(ii) Experiment 2. The same result is obtained because the same amounts of magnesium and acid are present. The reaction takes slightly longer when water is added.

(d) The graph is steeper because magnesium powder has a larger surface area. Only half of the hydrogen is produced (dotted line on Figure 6.11).

14(a) Your diagram should look like the one in Figure 6.12.

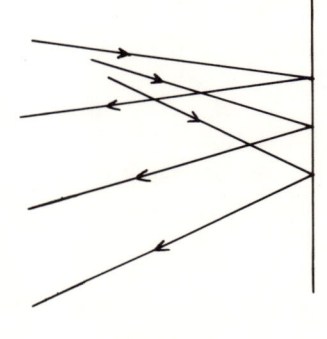

(b)

	Angle of incidence	Angle of reflection
ray 1	21°	21°
ray 2	32°	32°
ray 3	41°	41°

Fig. 6.12

(c) For each pair the angles of incidence and reflection are equal.

(d) Because of the way in which the rays spread out, it may be difficult to mark their positions precisely. Also, measurement of angles with a protractor may not be possible to better than within 1°. It may be better to move the lamp further from the mirror.

(e) Your tracing back to find the image point and lamp position should look like Figure 6.13.

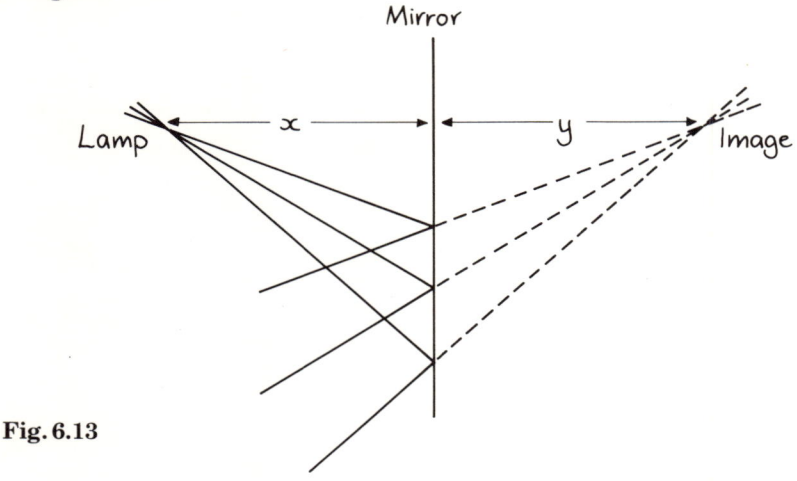

Fig. 6.13

If you measure the shortest distances to the mirror from the lamp and the image, marked *x* and *y* in the diagram, these distances should be the same.

(f) Figure 6.14 shows a suitable way of doing this. This arrangement is called a periscope.

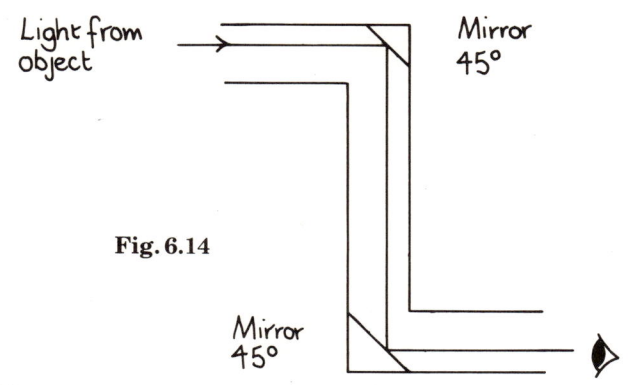

Fig. 6.14

15(a) and (b)
Between 2 and 7   38 mm
         7 and 11 46 mm
         11 and 15 56 mm
         15 and 20 68 mm
         20 and 28 84 mm
After 28 April   96 mm

(c) See Figure 6.15.

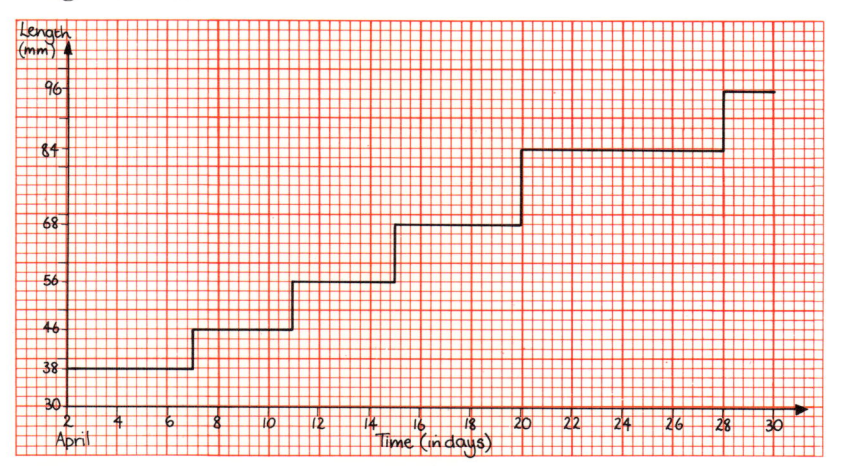

Fig. 6.15

(d) The locust is an insect and has an exoskeleton. This does not stretch as an animal grows so it sheds the exoskeleton when it moults. A new, larger one, grows underneath the old one and replaces it.

(e) Length of head, thorax, abdomen; wing size, antennae length; body mass.

(f) Temperature, availability of food and water.

16(a)

	Average length (in mm)	
	shoot	root
light	24.8	45.9
dark	33.7	47.4

(b) Light reduces the amount of growth of the shoot. The average difference between the two treatments = 8.9 mm.

(c) Light has no or little effect on root growth. The average difference = 1.5 mm.

(d)

	A	B
Number of leaves	2	2
Length of stem	15 mm	21 mm
Colour of leaf	green	yellow
Colour of stem	green	white
Length of root	10 mm	15 mm

> *At least ten seedlings must be used to eliminate individual differences.*

(e) Germinate three sets of cress seeds. Place one in a box with light from one side. Place another in a box and keep it in the dark. Place the third with illumination from all sides. Record the appearance of the seedlings every day for a week. The degree of bending can be measured against a protractor. All conditions, such as temperature, ought to be kept constant.

A clinostat is often used as a control for this experiment. A Petri dish with seedlings growing on blotting paper can be placed on this revolving drum which turns once every fifteen minutes. These seedlings will continue to grow vertically, they do not show a positive phototropic response to light coming from one side.

17(a) See Figure 6.16.

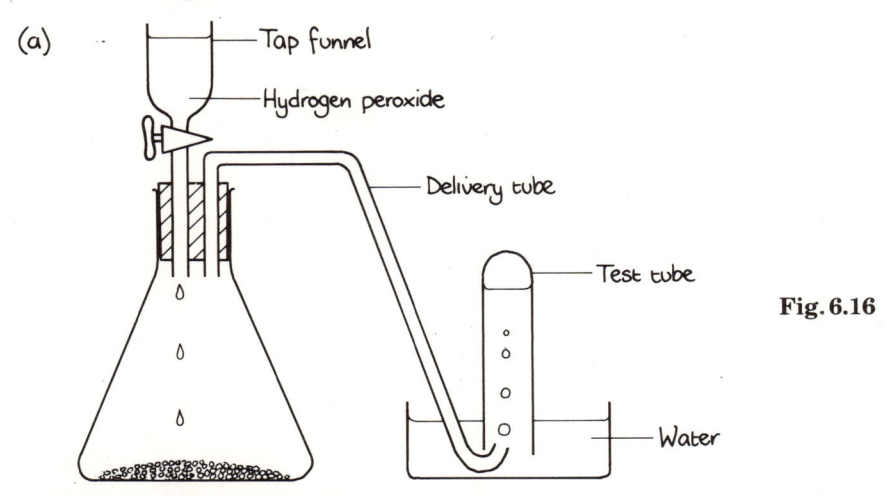

(a)

Fig. 6.16

(b) The first test tubes of gas collected will contain air pushed out of the apparatus. To ensure that no air is present in the oxygen collected, disregard the first test tubes of gas collected.

(c)(i) Metal oxides are solids, non-metal oxides are often gases.

(ii)

Element	pH of solution	Acidity/alkalinity
A	8	weak alkali
B	7	neutral
C	5	weak acid
D	11 – 14	strong alkali
E	1 – 3	strong acid
F	9	weak alkali

> *Students frequently make mathematical mistakes with indices. Remember*
> $$1\ mA = \frac{1}{1000}\ A$$
> $$= 0.001\ A$$
> $$= 10^{-3}\ A.$$

(iii)

	pH of oxide	Acidity/alkalinity
Metals	7 or above	neutral or alkali
Non-metals	below 7	acidic

(iv) D, F, A, B

(v) The more reactive the metal, the higher the pH or the more strongly alkaline the oxide solution is.

18(a) Any of the following:
Temperature; mass (or volume) of water; mass of powder; type of cloth stained; amount of grass stain; amount of stirring; length of washing time.

> *Testing for starch with iodine solution is the basis of many science assessments.*

(b) Stained cloths, two beakers, water bath or apparatus to keep water warm, two thermometers, two stirring rods, clock, balance to weigh out powder, measuring cylinder.

(c) Stain several pieces of cloth evenly with grass. Weigh out equal masses of X and Y. Add to equal volumes of water in beakers.
Mix and bring solutions to the washing temperature in the water bath. Add cloth to beakers containing X and Y, stir and leave for a fixed length of time.
Remove, dry and compare stains.
You should appreciate the need for a fair comparison. If you are aiming at higher grades you should appreciate the need for repetition, varying conditions and a method for objective comparison of the results perhaps against colour standards.

19(a) To make sure that there was no starch already in the leaves before putting the plant in the light.

(b) Put the leaves in a boiling tube with some ethanol. Heat the boiling tube in a bath of hot water. Switch off naked flames as ethanol is highly flammable (Figure 6.17).

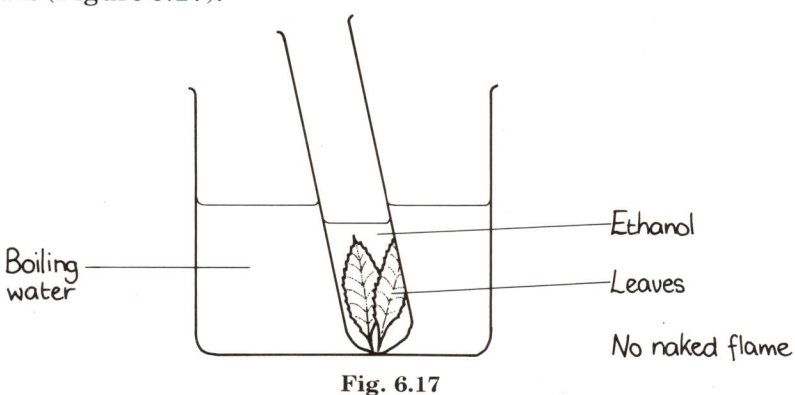

Fig. 6.17

(c) Spread leaves on a white tile. Add several drops of iodine solution and allow them to soak into the leaves.

(d) The leaves have produced starch in the light but not in the dark, so light is needed for starch production.

Starch is only found in the green parts of the leaf so it is either produced or stored here only. (It is not strictly valid to conclude that chlorophyll, the green colouring matter, is needed for starch to be produced from this evidence alone.)

20 Before coming up with a design you should have thought about some of the following problem areas:

- how to compare the energy given out when the sample burns
- how to minimize the energy lost to the surroundings
- how to make sure that each sample burns completely.

The first student has tried to overcome some of these problems (Figure 6.18).

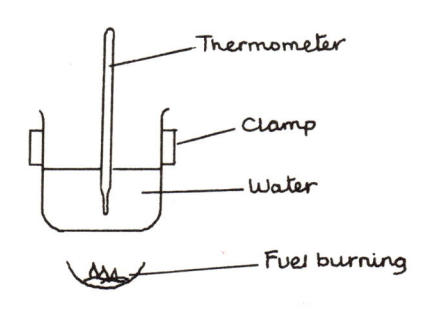

Fig. 6.18

Put 100 cm³ of water in a beaker with a thermometer. Put the fuel in a crucible as close up to the beaker of water as you can get it. Then light the fuel. Whilst it is burning stir the water gently. Find the highest temperature the water gets to. Then work out the temperature rise by taking away the starting temperature of the water.
Repeat the experiment with other fuels, and see which gives the greatest temperature rise. This is the one with the highest energy value.

The next student has tried to overcome more of the difficulties, and even designed a simple piece of equipment to do the job. This is obviously a better answer (Figure 6.19).

> Take an old soup can. With the top and bottom removed, cut the top rim of the can into strips so that it can be bent to support a small beaker. Cut some slots out of the bottom to allow air to be drawn in. Put it on a heat-proof mat.
>
> *(diagram showing beaker on top of old soup can with crucible of fuel inside)*
>
> Put the fuel into a suitable crucible which will slide into the can through one of the slots. Measure 100 cm³ of cold water into the beaker and measure the temperature of the water. Use a match or Bunsen burner to start the fuel burning and then slide the crucible into position. Stir the water gently with a thermometer and measure the highest temperature reached.
> Repeat using the other fuels in turn, ensuring the starting temperature of the water is the same in each case. It is important to keep the energy lost to the surroundings as small as possible. If one of the fuels takes longer to burn than the others this will have to be taken into account when drawing up a conclusion.
> If they all take the same time to burn, then the one which causes the highest rise in temperature has the greatest energy value.

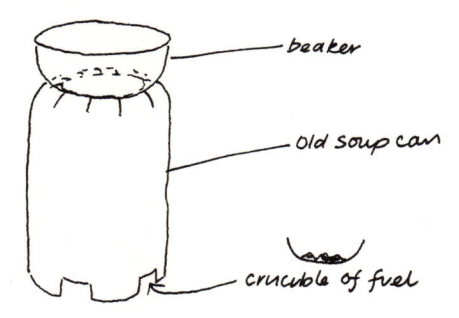

Fig. 6.19

21(a) Sterilizing the bottle kills any bacteria or wild yeasts that are on the surface of pieces of equipment, such as the bottle and the bung. If these grow in the sugar solution they may compete with the yeast for food and also alter the flavour of any drink that is produced by fermentation.

(b) This kills any bacteria or wild yeasts in the solution; it is necessary to cool the solution before adding the yeast because yeast would die if put into hot water.

(c) As a source of food for the yeast.

(d) A gas, carbon dioxide, is produced by the yeast. If the fermenter is airtight, the gas cannot escape so that the pressure builds up and this eventually breaks the bottle.

(e) This allows carbon dioxide to escape but stops bacteria or wild yeasts from entering. It also excludes oxygen.

(f) Fit a delivery tube to the bottle; place the end of the tube into a test tube containing limewater. The limewater turns milky.

(g) Yeast respires faster at a medium (warm) temperature; fermentation occurs more rapidly at a higher temperature.

NB Yeast is not a bacterium. Yeasts are fungi, they have nuclei with chromosomes. Bacteria have no nuclei and do *not* have chromosomes like those found in yeasts, green plants and animals.

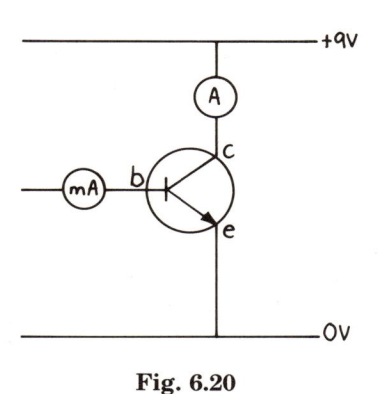

22(a) See Figure 6.20.
(b) See Figure 6.21.

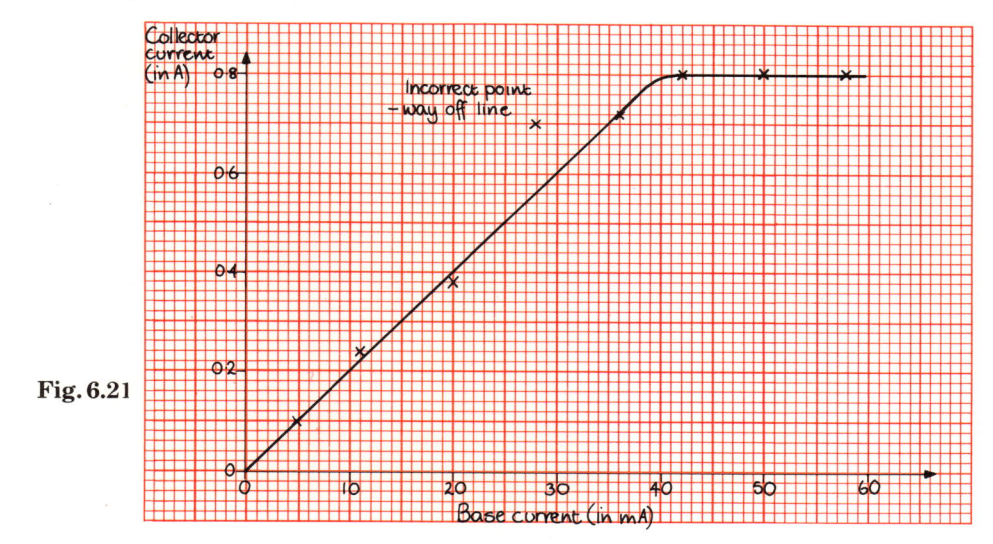

Fig. 6.20

Fig. 6.21

Notice how the line starts straight and then levels off at a collector current of 0.8 A.

The point which does not fit in with the rest is the fourth one (collector current 0.70 A and base current 28 mA).

(c) 33 mA. This is found by drawing a straight line *across* from 0.67 A on the collector current axis to where it meets the graph line, then drawing a straight line down from this point to the base current axis.

(d) The values for the current gain are; from the top, 20.0, 21.8, 19.5 (ignore this one), 20.0, 19.0, 16.0, 13.8.

(e) The current gain keeps the same value (about 20) until the collector current reaches 0.8 A. Further increases in the base current cause no increase in the collector current, and so the gain is reduced.

23 Put some water into the measuring cylinder until it is about one third full. Take the volume reading.

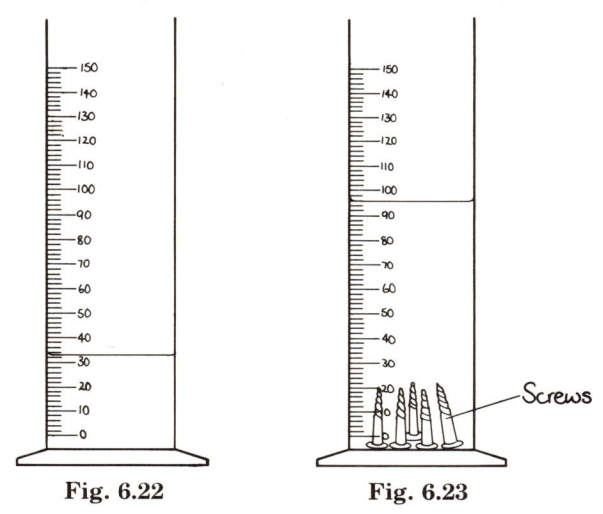

Fig. 6.22   Fig. 6.23

Add the screws one by one, taking care not to splash the water out. Put them all in if they will go. Read the new volume.

To find the volume of all the screws, take the volume of the water away from the total volume.

e.g. volume of screws = 96 cm^3 − 33 cm^3
= 63 cm^3

Now divide by the number of screws (50 in this case) to find the average volume of a single screw.

e.g. volume of 1 screw = 63/50 = 1.26 cm^3

24(a) The reading on the forcemeter is 23 N.
g.p.e. gained by brick = 23 N × 0.8 m
= 18.4 J

(b) The reading on the forcemeter is 17 N.
Energy used by Tracey = 17 N × 2.2 m
= 37.4 J

This is more than the energy gained by the brick and the ramp, due to movement against the friction force between them.

(c) Efficiency of pulling the brick up

$$= \frac{\text{energy gained by brick}}{\text{energy used by Tracey}}$$

$$= \frac{18.4}{37.4}$$

$$= 0.49$$

(d) The reading on the forcemeter is 12 N.

(e) Energy used to pull trolley up = 12 N × 2.2 m
= 26.4 J

Efficiency $= \frac{18.4}{26.4}$

$= 0.70$

(f) The trolley method is more efficient. This is because, even though the trolley is extra mass to be lifted up, there is much less friction than when the brick was just dragged up.

25 Testing Tom's hypothesis

Requires:
- That the water in the vessel is heated but sunlight is omitted.
- A means of measuring the volume of air formed, e.g. counting the number of bubbles or an upturned measuring cylinder in water.
- A means of maintaining the water at a constant temperature over a range of temperatures, e.g. water bath together with thermometer.

The vessel is heated, to say, 40 °C, 60 °C and 80 °C. Total volume of air collected is measured.

Testing Jerry's hypothesis

Requires:
- That light shines on the water in a vessel but the heating effect is eliminated, e.g. allow sun to shine on the vessel but continuously cool the vessel to maintain constant temperature.
- A means of measuring the volume of air formed, e.g. counting the number of bubbles or an upturned measuring cylinder in water.
- Clock required to record length of time sunlight falls.

Allow light to shine continuously and record volume of gas collected at one hourly intervals.

The apparatus in Figure 6.24 would be suitable for these experiments.

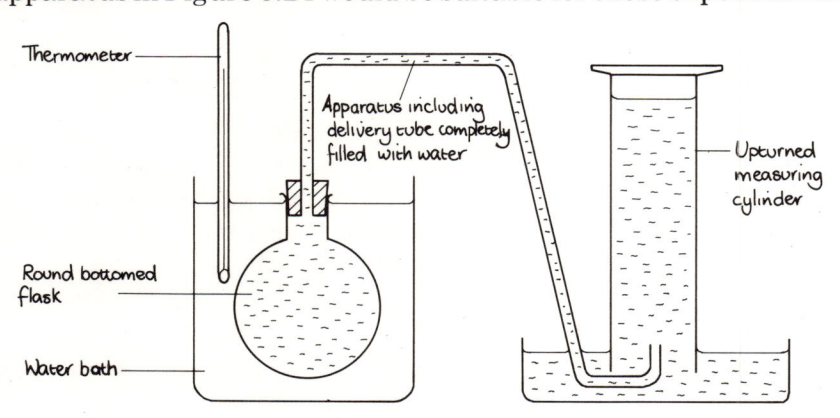

Fig. 6.24

26(a) Nitrogen, carbon dioxide.
(b) See Figure 6.25.

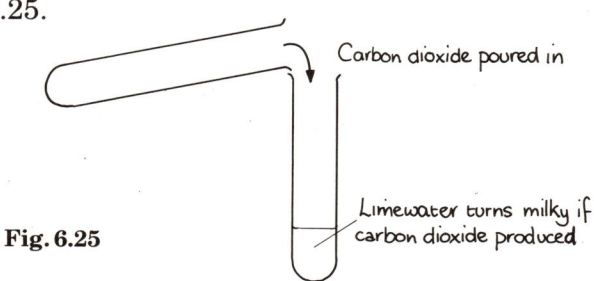

Fig. 6.25

Carbon dioxide poured in
Limewater turns milky if carbon dioxide produced

27(a) To saturate the water with dissolved oxygen. Any oxygen produced during the experiment could not then dissolve in the water.
(b) Carbon dioxide is needed for photosynthesis.
(c) To ensure accurate measurement. The narrow tube magnifies the length of the bubble produced.
(d) 5 cm.
(e) It decreases.
(f) Temperature. The beaker of water prevents a temperature rise by providing a large volume of water.
(g) See Figure 6.26.

Fig. 6.26

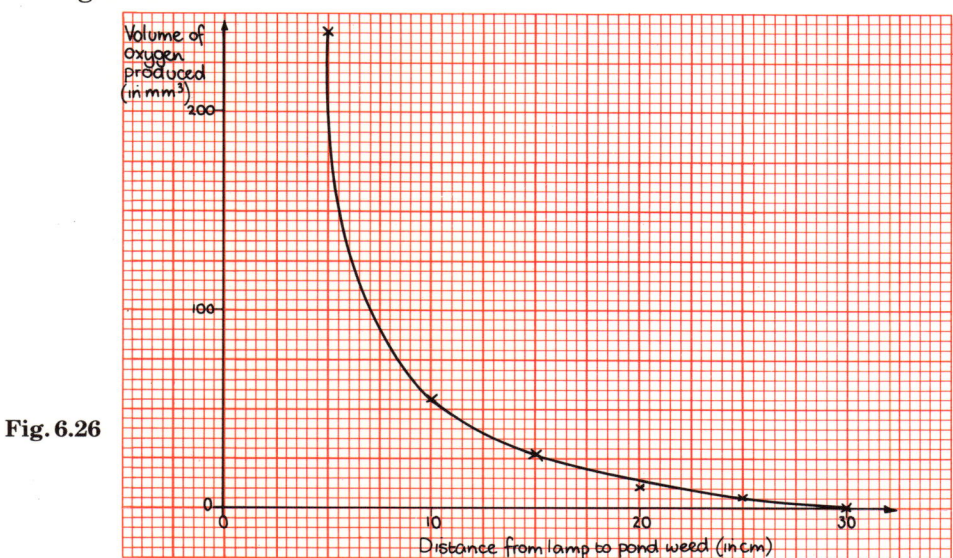

(h) Light energy is needed for photosynthesis. As light intensity increases the rate of photosynthesis increases and therefore the rate of oxygen production.

28(a)

Soil	Volume drained (in cm^3)
clay	2
loam	23
sand	30

(b) Much of the water stays in the air spaces and sticks to the particles. Even in the sand not all will drain through.

(c)

Soil	Height of water after	
	8 hours (in cm)	3 days (in cm)
clay	4	42
loam	14	28
sand	20	21

(d) Water drains through sand much faster than clay. For loam it is somewhere in between. Water soaks up through sand by capillary action quite rapidly at first, but eventually not as *far* as in clay.

29(a)

Time (in hours)	Number of yeast cells
0	30
1	28
2	32
3	43
4	75
5	127

(b) See Figure 6.27.

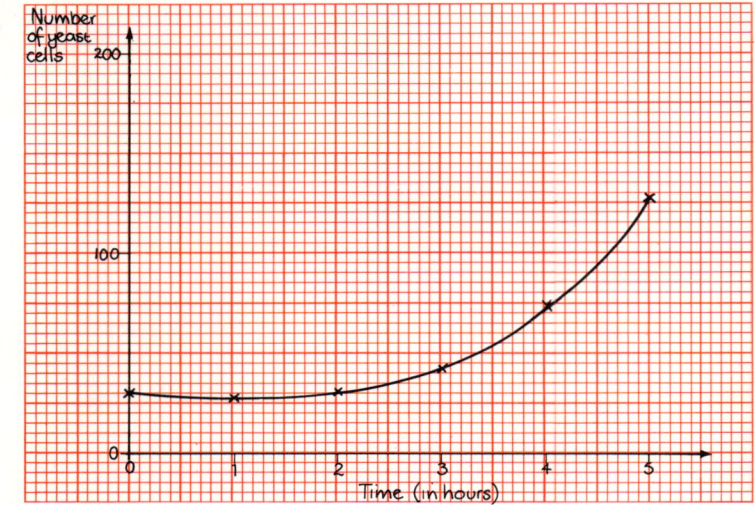

Fig. 6.27

(c) The effect of random sampling.

(d) Rapid increase in population for several hours, followed by slowing down and eventual fall as nutrients are exhausted, toxins accumulate, etc.

30(a)

Sector of leaf	Number of aphids	
	in wind	after wind
1	7	5
2	10	7
3	9	6
4	14	7
5	7	8
6	4	4
Total	51	37

(b) In A the aphids are concentrated near the base of the leaf and close to the veins. In B they are quite evenly spaced.

(c)(i) Some aphids have flown away to other leaves, perhaps to more exposed parts of the tree or the other side of the leaf.

(ii) There are several possible answers. In high winds the base of the leaf will flap less than the ends and be more secure. The raised veins may also provide shelter.

31 There are several approaches to this question.

Fig. 6.28 Wrap some thin insulating wire around the iron bar and then connect the ends of the wire to a 4V d.c. electrical supply. Switch on the electricity and use the magnet formed to pick up an iron bar. Pull the two bars apart.
Switch off the electricity and wind twice as many turns of wire around the bar. Switch on again and pick up the iron bar as before. Now see if it is harder to pull the bars apart this time.

This method used in Figure 6.28 solves the problem but it relies upon a judgment of whether or not it is harder to pull apart the two iron bars. The example in Figure 6.29 is much better.

> One end of a metre length of insulated copper wire was connected to the positive terminal of the 4 V d.c. power supply. The wire was then wrapped five times around the iron bar. The other end of the wire was attached to the negative terminal.
>
> The bar was then clamped horizontally so that weights could be hung from a weight hanger at the other end of the bar.
>
> [Diagram: clamp holding iron bar wrapped with coil of wire, with weight hanger held by magnetic forces at the far end.]
>
> The weight hanger is made of steel and is held by magnetic forces onto the iron bar when an electric current was passing.
>
> Weights were added to the weight hanger until it fell off. The weight required for the weight hanger to fall off was noted.
>
> The experiment was repeated several times, each time increasing the number of turns by five. The results can be recorded in a table below.
>
> | Numbers of turns | Weight supported in g |
> |---|---|
> | 5 | |
> | 10 | |
> | 15 | |
> | 20 | |
>
> From these results it can be seen whether or not the number of turns of wire affect the strength of the magnet.

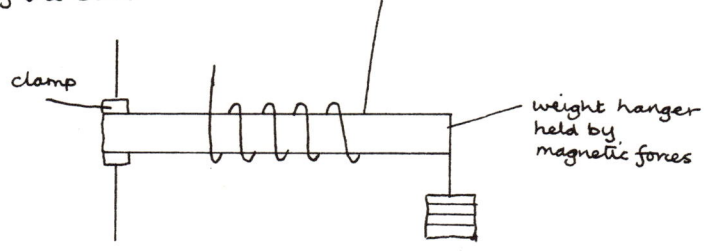

Fig. 6.29

32(a) A teat pipette or burette.

(b) B

(c) A

(d) B

(e) Find the mass of a suitable vessel e.g. watch glass, beaker, etc. Add the substance to the vessel until the mass has increased by 1.50 g.
OR
Find the mass of a suitable vessel. Set the tare on the balance. Add the substance until the reading is 1.50 g.

(f) It increases the hardness.

(g)

Substance added	Effect on temporary hardness	Effect on permanent hardness
bath cubes	removes/softens	removes/softens
salt	no effect	no effect
slaked lime	removes	no effect

(h) So that the amount of hardness present was the same to start with in both investigations, and therefore a fair comparison could be made.
(i) There are several possibilities. Three of these are shown in Figure 6.30.

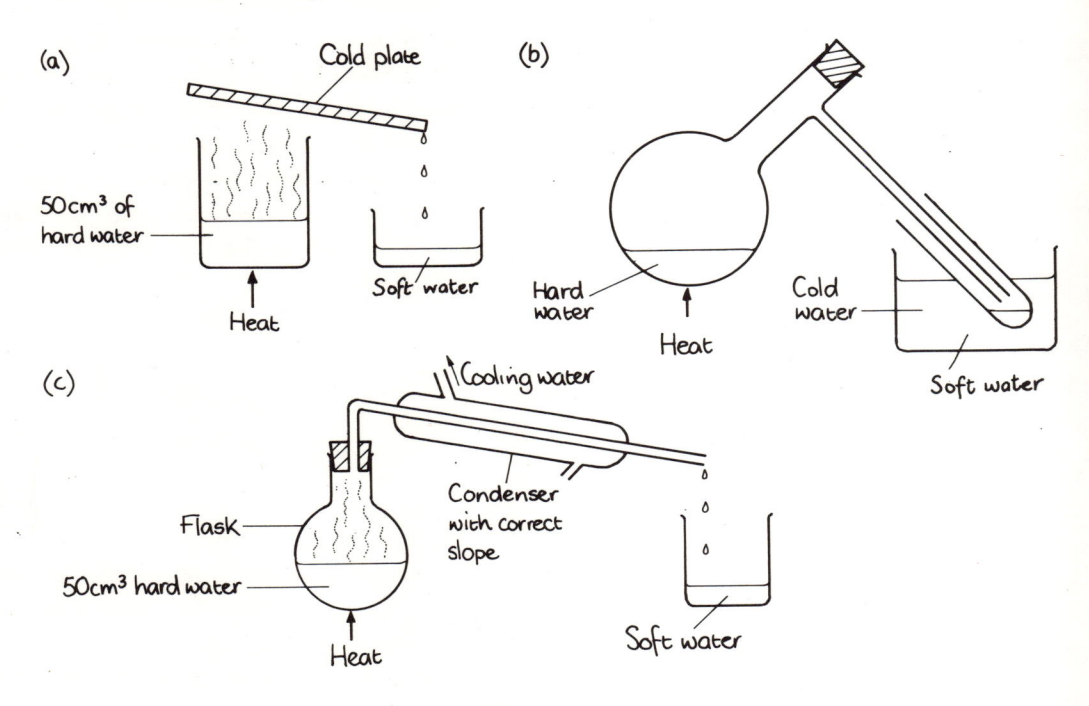

Fig. 6.30

In (a) only a small amount of pure water would be obtained and the experimenter would finish up with scalded hands! In (b) more pure water would be collected but some steam would not condense. The best method is (c) where the steam is condensed using a condenser. The condenser must slope downward.

33 A lorry on a steep hill could be modelled by a trolley on a sloping runway. As an alternative you could use a roller skate and a plank of wood (Figure 6.31).

Fig. 6.31

The mass can be changed by taping separate masses onto the trolley or skate. The accelerations can be compared by two methods.

One method is to use a ticker timer to record the motion of the 'lorry' as it goes down the hill. An alternative way is to use optical gates linked to a timer to measure the speed of the trolley at two different points. The essential features of one of these methods should appear on your diagram.

Procedure:

The lorry should be released from a marked position on the hill. Three or four runs should be attempted from the same point.

Masses are added to the lorry until double the mass of the original lorry is reached. The experiment is repeated keeping all conditions the same.

Conclusion:

Ticker timer method The accelerations can be compared by comparing the tape traces obtained.

Optical gate method If the optical gates are linked to a computer, the accelerations can be displayed directly on a screen. If the optical gates are only attached to a timer, the acceleration can be calculated using the equation:

$$\text{acceleration} = \frac{\text{increase in velocity}}{\text{time taken for velocity increase}}$$

34(a)(*i*) measuring cylinder.
(*ii*) A teat pipette.
(b) A control. Compare the rate of corrosion with and without inhibitors to see if inhibitors have any effect.
(c) Inhibitor B.
(d) B, A, D, C
(e) It increases the rate of corrosion above that where there is no inhibitor.
(f) Take five pieces of steel of similar size. Make a 20 per cent solution of inhibitor B. Using a measuring cylinder, add 100 cm³ of the solution to each of five beakers. Add five drops of test reagent. Using a water bath/oven/electric heater, heat solutions to, say, 30 °C, 45 °C, 55 °C, 65 °C and 80 °C to give a wide range of temperatures. Use thermometers to measure temperatures. Maintain the beakers at these temperatures for four months, making observations at monthly intervals.

Central heating systems operate over this range of temperature and inhibitors must work over the range of temperature.

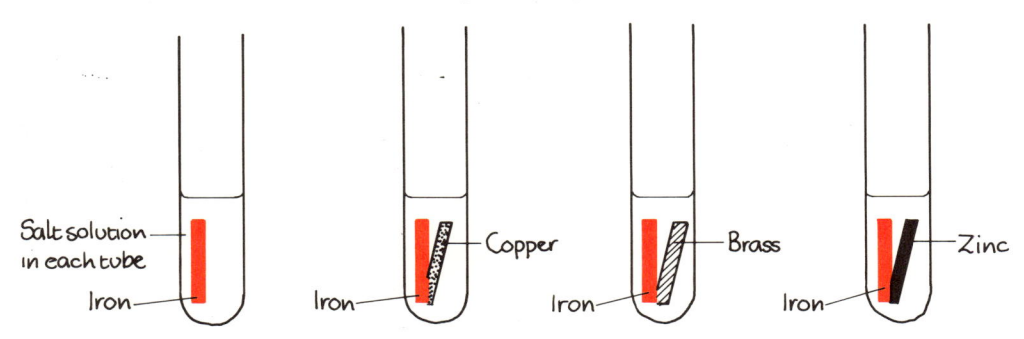

Fig. 6.32

(g) Test tubes were set up as in Figure 6.32. In each test tube was an identical salt solution. Five drops of test reagent were added to each test tube. In test tube 1 there was iron alone. In test tube 2 iron was *in contact with* copper. In test tube 3 iron was *in contact with* brass. In test tube 4 iron was *in contact with* zinc. The test tubes were looked at regularly.

The solutions in test tubes 2 and 3 should turn blue before the solution in test tube 1. The solution in test tube 4 may not turn blue. If it does it would take much longer.

35 Rusting uses up oxygen in test tube B. This test tube therefore contains much less oxygen than test tube A. Other conditions are the same. The fact that the seeds in B did not germinate suggests that oxygen is needed for the germination of seeds.

36(a) Any of the following.
Moving away from light; moving to greater humidity; odour of dead plant; touching against both sides of a tube; climbing upwards away from gravity.

(b) Answers should concentrate on measuring the two factors separately and providing controlled conditions in a choice chamber.

For example, set up a choice chamber with a crushed petal or paper soaked in petal juice on one side and an equivalent counterpart on the other. Petals, etc. should not be visible, so the experiment could be run in the dark. Several earwigs should be used and several runs done. Count numbers going towards the scent each time.

> *The decomposition of hydrogen peroxide into water and oxygen is frequently used in chemistry in rate of reaction experiments.*

37(a) See Figure 6.33.

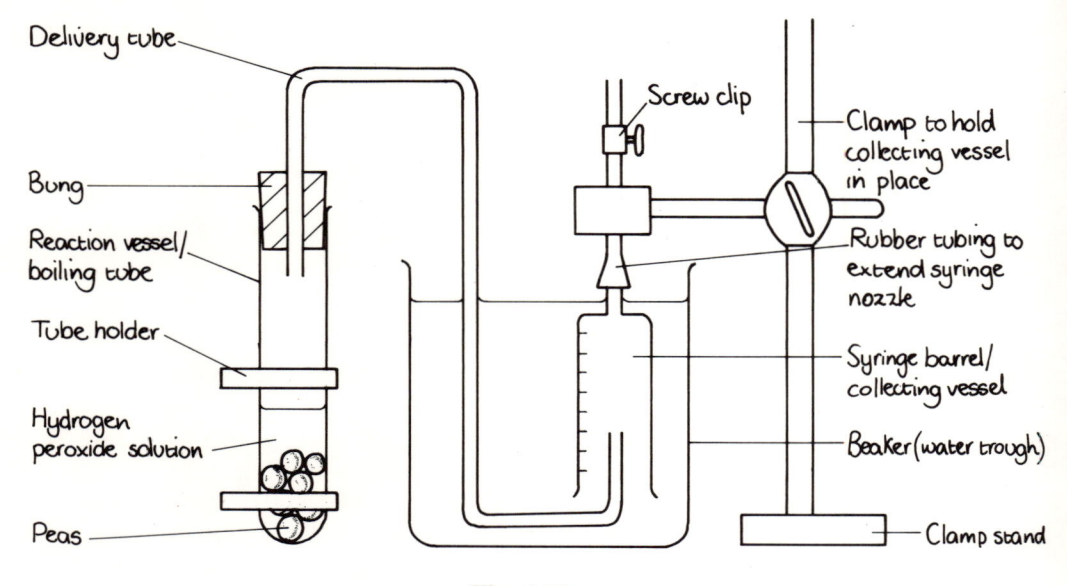

Fig. 6.33

(Diagram labels: Delivery tube; Bung; Reaction vessel/boiling tube; Tube holder; Hydrogen peroxide solution; Peas; Screw clip; Clamp to hold collecting vessel in place; Rubber tubing to extend syringe nozzle; Syringe barrel/collecting vessel; Beaker (water trough); Clamp stand)

(b) One with no peas; boiled peas used instead of the germinating peas.

(c) To measure the volume of gas produced.

(d) Add the germinating peas to hydrogen peroxide; when the first bubble of gas is released into the syringe barrel start timing; note the volume of gas collected after each minute for five minutes.

(e) Temperature Place the boiling tube into a water bath. Keep the temperature of the water bath constant at 10 °C. Collect the gas as before. Repeat the experiment using fresh hydrogen peroxide and fresh peas at 20 °C, 30 °C and 40 °C.

pH Add dilute acid or alkali to the reaction mixture, repeat the experiment making sure that the temperature is kept constant at, say, 20 °C, by using a water bath. Test the pH by using a pH meter or Universal indicator.

When investigating the effect of one condition, it is important to keep all other variables constant. When investigating temperature, the pH should be kept constant; when investigating pH, the temperature should be kept constant.

38(a) Y. The bottom of the meniscus should be level with the line on the pipette.

(b) B: 1 g per dm^3
C: 0.1 g per dm^3
D: 0.01 g per dm^3

(c) Stir solution A thoroughly. Measure out 10 cm^3 of solution A into a graduated flask with a 10 cm^3 pipette (Figure 6.34). Add distilled water until the bottom of meniscus is on the line on the flask. Shake the flask thoroughly. Shaking or stirring solutions is to make sure that the solution is the same throughout.

(d) To ensure that all test tubes are heated to the same temperature.

(e)(*i*) A small measuring cylinder, small syringe or graduated pipette.
(*ii*) A teat pipette.

(f) 0.1 g per dm^3.

(g) Make up a dilution series between 0.1 and 0.01 g per dm^3 and repeat the Benedict's test with these solutions.

(h) Place the test tubes into a water bath. Wear safety goggles.

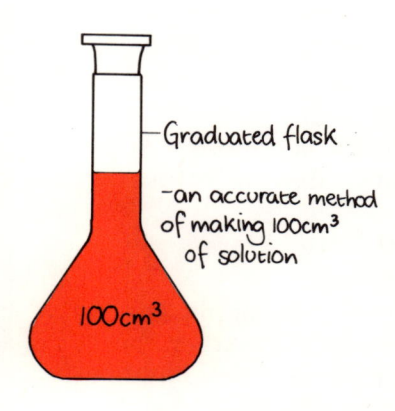

Fig. 6.34 — Graduated flask — an accurate method of making 100 cm^3 of solution (100 cm^3)

(i) Make up four pieces of apparatus as shown in Figure 6.35. Place each one in a water bath at a constant temperature (e.g. 10 °C, 20 °C, 30 °C, 40 °C).

Visking tubing — Rubber band — Glucose solution
Boiling tube — Water — Visking tubing tied at the bottom

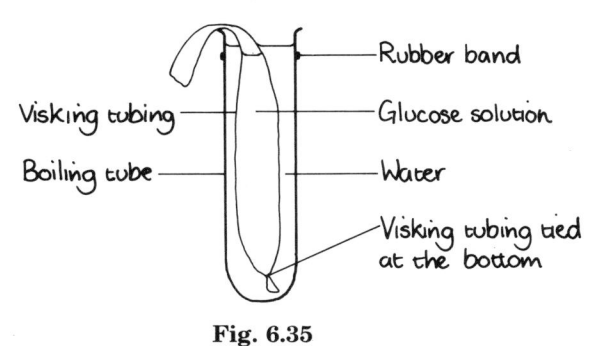

Fig. 6.35

Take samples with a teat pipette from the water surrounding the tubing every two minutes. Test these samples with Benedict's solution and record the time take for green cloudiness to appear. The concentration of glucose in the water should increase with time so it is possible to compare this increase in concentration for each temperature used.

(j) Prepare a solution of potassium manganate(VII) of 1 g per dm^3. Dilute this solution successively as before. Each time put some of the solution into a clean test tube and hold it up against a white tile. Continue doing this until no pink colour remains.

The fact that the solution is still pink even when very dilute suggests that the particles making up potassium manganate(VII) are very small indeed.

39(a) Water.

(b) An accurate balance reading to 0.01 g is not required as weighings are only to the nearest 5 g. A compression spring balance or a lever arm balance would be suitable.

(c) All the water had evaporated and there was no further change in mass.

(d) 200 g.

(e) $\frac{200 \times 100\%}{1000} = 20\%$

(f) In the first hour the composts were still warming up from room temperature.

(g) Humus formed from decaying plant and animal matter – organic matter.

(h) A measuring cylinder.

(i) Compost A contains more air or is less tightly packed and retains less water.

(j) Acidity/alkalinity of the soil.

(k) Blueberries.

40(a) Ethanol, like any flammable liquid, should not be heated directly by a Bunsen burner flame. It can be heated by placing the test tube in a beaker of hot water.

(b) It removes the chlorophyll from the leaf so that the colour of the iodine can be clearly seen. Ethanol decolourizes the leaf. You may remember that ethanol is used to extract the coloured plant pigments from grass in a simple chromatography experiment. It is also used to remove grass stains.

(c) To soften it so that the ethanol can penetrate the cells easily.

(d) Wear safety goggles. Light a Bunsen burner and boil a beaker half full of water. (Alternatively, half fill the beaker with boiling water from a kettle.)

When the water boils, detach a leaf from the plant and, using forceps, put the leaf into boiling water for one minute. Then turn off the Bunsen burner flame.

Transfer the leaf to a test tube containing ethanol and place this into the water bath.

Wait until the leaf has lost its green colour and gone white. When this has happened remove the test tube from the water bath and take the leaf out of the test tube.

Put the leaf into the beaker of hot water for a few seconds.

Spread the leaf out on a white tile and cover it with iodine solution. Leave for a few minutes to allow the iodine to soak into the leaf. Observe the colour of the iodine solution.

(e) Take two potted plants of the same species. Place one in the dark and the other in the light for one week. Remove a leaf from each after a week and test as outlined in **(d)** above.

The leaf from the dark should stain yellow with iodine showing there is no starch present.

The leaf from the light should stain black with iodine, showing starch is present.

While the leaves are in the dark, only respiration occurs. There is no photosynthesis. Thus all of the stored starch is used up by respiration. This process is called destarching. It is a good idea to start all experiments which show that something is needed for photosynthesis (e.g. light, carbon dioxide and chlorophyll) with destarched leaves.

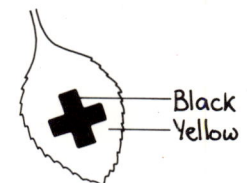

Alternatively, you could place a stencil over a leaf and leave the plant in the light for a week (Figure 6.36). Test for starch as outlined above.

Fig. 6.36

41(a) A metal – good heat conductor and high melting point. Of the metals copper is probably best.

(b) To prevent heat loss/to act as insulation.

(c) To stop the flame blowing out.
To prevent heat losses.
To prevent uneven heat losses. (*Best answer*)

(d) 100 g. Remember, 1 cm^3 of water has a mass of 1 g. It is often more convenient to measure out liquids by volume than by mass.

(e) 19 °C

(f) See Figure 6.37.

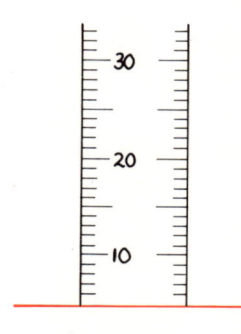

Fig. 6.37

(g) A: 0.71 g of fuel used.
B: 0.58 g of fuel used.
C: 0.65 g of fuel used.

Each time the same amount of energy was produced because the same mass of water was heated to the same temperature rise. Therefore, fuel B produces most energy per gram.

(h) Heat produced = mass of water × temperature rise × specific heat capacity

Heat produced = 100 × 9 × 4.2
= 3780 J

(i) Only a comparison is being made. Heat losses will be the same for each fuel.

(j) Attempt to calculate the heat gained by container X and the thermometer. Cover the container. Use a larger mass of water and a smaller temperature rise. The apparatus in Figure 6.38 could be used. This apparatus minimizes heat losses.

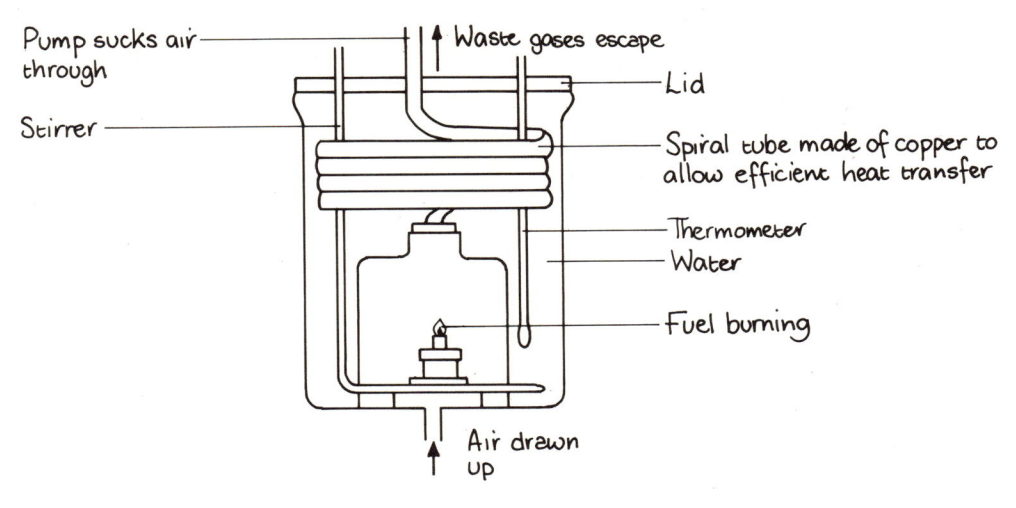

Fig. 6.38

(k) *(i)* A measuring cylinder, a burette.

(ii) Measure the volume of fuel put into burner at the start. Burn to achieve a 10 °C temperature rise. Empty remaining fuel into a burette to find volume remaining.

OR

Look up the density of fuel in a data book and calculate volumes.

$$\text{volume} = \frac{\text{mass}}{\text{density}}$$

Use results from the original investigation.

(iii)

	Fuel A	Fuel B	Fuel C
1st volume			
2nd volume			

(iv) The fuel requiring the least volume of fuel supplies the most heat per cubic centimetre.

42(a) To avoid the forces of adhesion between the ruler and the bench along the whole length of the ruler.

(b) See Figure 6.39 (overleaf).

(c) *(i)* 85.5 g *(ii)* 105.0 g

(d) Here are three qualities of answer.

(1) The further away from the hinge the string loop is the less mass is added *just* to lift the ruler.

(2) The further away from the hinge the loop is the less mass is needed *just* to lift the ruler. The changes do not go up in regular steps.

(3) The mass required to raise the ruler is inversely proportional to the distance the loop is from the hinge.

i.e. position × mass = constant
$$50 \times 120 = 6000$$
$$54 \times 110 = 5940$$
$$60 \times 100 = 6000 \text{ etc.}$$

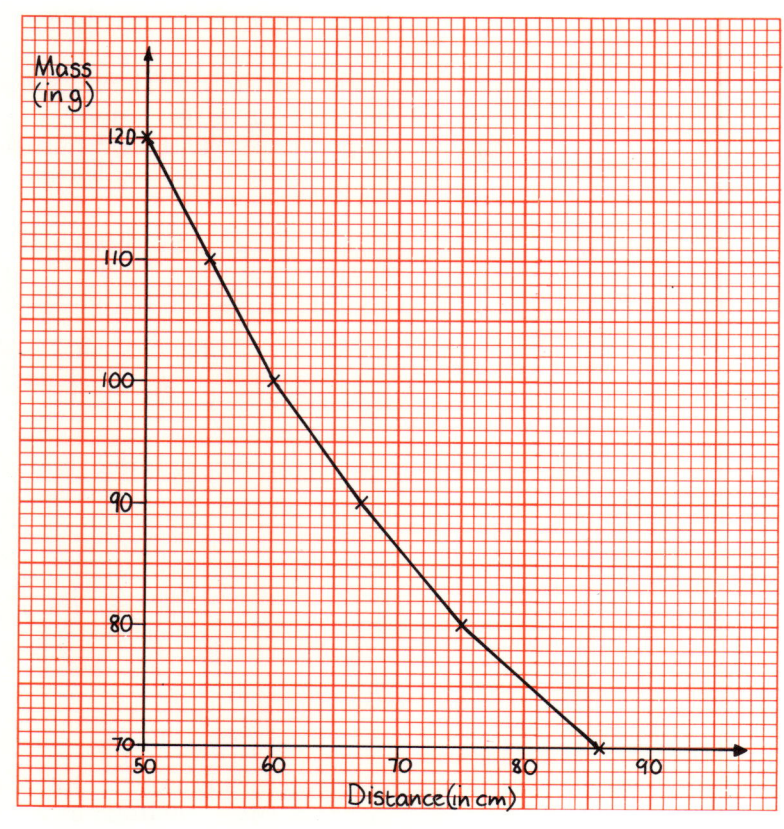

Fig. 6.39

As you can see, all three answers are correct but from (*1*) to (*3*) they are increasingly *scientifically* expressed and as a result worthy of increasing marks.

43(a) The voltmeter is connected in parallel with the LDR. The milliammeter is connected in series.

(b) Smaller pin-holes would let in less light, bigger pin-holes would let in more light. This would affect the resistance in the same way as moving the torch.

(c) 0.0024 A   1667 Ω
       0.0028 A   1429 Ω
       0.0032 A   1250 Ω
       0.0035 A   1143 Ω
       0.0037 A   1081 Ω

(d) Your scale should be 1 cm for every hole on the *x*-axis and 1 cm for 100 Ω on the *y*-axis. Note the lowest reading on the *y*-axis should be 1000 Ω (as there are no readings below this value), not 0 Ω.
The points should be joined together with a smooth curve. The graph should look like Figure 6.40.

(e) Again here are three possible answers to this question.
(*1*) The more light on the LDR the lower the resistance becomes.
(*2*) The greater the light level on the LDR the lower the resistance becomes but the change does not go down in regular steps.
(*3*) The greater the light level on the LDR the lower the resistance becomes. The change is not linear (regular steps) and is not inversely proportional (i.e. no. of holes × resistance does not equal a constant).
Again these answers are worthy of increasing marks.

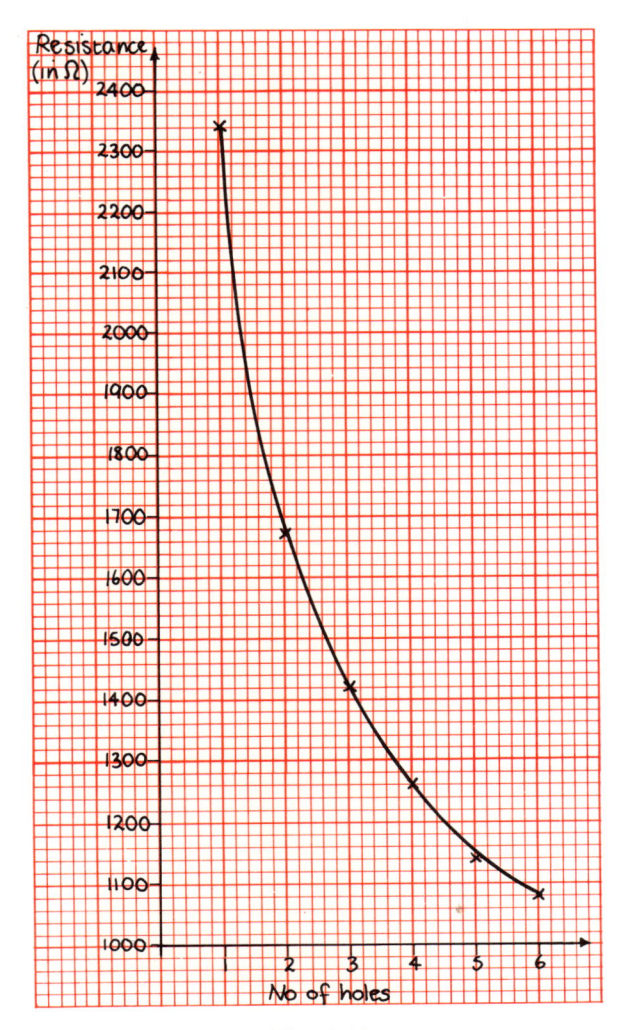

Fig. 6.40

44(a) To set the pH meter. Before use the pH meter has to be set against a known standard pH solution called a buffer solution.
(b) Indicators using colour are unreliable with strongly coloured solutions.
(c)(i) From the top yellow; green; colourless; red.
(ii) Methyl orange.
(iii) pH 7

45(a) Only potassium hydroxide.
(b) Zinc hydroxide, lead(II) hydroxide, aluminium hydroxide.
(c) Add sodium hydroxide solution to separate solutions containing iron(II) ions and iron(III) ions. With iron(II) ions a dirty dark green precipitate is formed. With iron(II) ions an orange/brown precipitate is formed.
(d) The reactions of sodium hydroxide solution and ammonia solution with copper(II) sulphate solution can be used. Put samples of copper(II) sulphate solution into two test tubes.

To each test tube add one of the unknown solutions drop by drop. The sodium hydroxide solution will precipitate a light blue solid (copper(II) hydroxide) which will not redissolve in excess. The ammonia solution will precipitate the same pale blue solid but this will dissolve in excess ammonia to produce a royal blue solution.

APPENDIX 1

Examination groups: addresses

LEAG – London and East Anglian Group

London	University of London Schools Examinations Board Stewart House, 32 Russell Square, London WC1B 5DN
LREB	London Regional Examinations Board Lyon House, 104 Wandsworth High Street, London SW18 4LF
EAEB	East Anglian Examinations Board The Lindens, Lexden Road, Colchester, Essex CO3 3RL (0206 549595)

MEG – Midlands Examining Group

Cambridge	University of Cambridge Local Examinations Syndicate Syndicate Buildings, 1 Hills Road, Cambridge CB1 2EU (0223 61111)
O & C	Oxford and Cambridge Schools Examinations Board 10 Trumpington Street, Cambridge CB2 1QB and Elsfield Way, Oxford OX2 8EP
SUJB	Southern Universities' Joint Board for School Examinations Cotham Road, Bristol BS6 6DD
WMEB	West Midlands Examinations Board Norfolk House, Smallbrook Queensway, Birmingham B5 4NJ
EMREB	East Midland Regional Examinations Board Robins Wood House, Robins Wood Road, Aspley, Nottingham NG8 3NR

NEA – Northern Examination Association (*write to your local board.*)

JMB	Joint Matriculation Board (061-273 2565) Devas Street, Manchester M15 6EU (*also for centres outside the NEA area*)
ALSEB	Associated Lancashire Schools Examining Board 12 Harter Street, Manchester M1 6HL
NREB	North Regional Examinations Board Wheatfield Road, Westerhope, Newcastle upon Tyne NE5 5JZ
NWREB	North-West Regional Examinations Board Orbit House, Albert Street, Eccles, Manchester M30 0WL
YHREB	Yorkshire and Humberside Regional Examinations Board Harrogate Office — 31–33 Springfield Avenue, Harrogate HG1 2HW Sheffield Office — Scarsdale House, 136 Derbyshire Lane, Sheffield S8 8SE

NISEC – Northern Ireland

NISEC	Northern Ireland Schools Examinations Council Beechill House, 42 Beechill Road, Belfast BT8 4RS (0232 704666)

SEB – Scotland

SEB	Scottish Examinations Board Ironmills Road, Dalkeith, Midlothian EH22 1BR (031-663 6601)

SEG – Southern Examining Group

AEB	The Associated Examining Board Stag Hill House, Guildford, Surrey GU2 5XJ (0483 503123)
Oxford	Oxford Delegacy of Local Examinations Ewert Place, Summertown, Oxford OX2 7BZ
SREB	Southern Regional Examinations Board Eastleigh House, Market Street, Eastleigh, Hampshire SO5 4SW
SEREB	South-East Regional Examinations Board Beloe House, 2–10 Mount Ephraim Road, Tunbridge Wells TN1 1EU
SWEB	South-Western Examinations Board 23–29 Marsh Street, Bristol BS1 4BP

WJEC – Wales

WJEC	Welsh Joint Education Committee 245 Western Avenue, Cardiff CF5 2YX (0222 561231)

(The boards to which you should write are underlined in each case.)

APPENDIX 2

Common apparatus

General laboratory glass and china ware
Figure 1 contains drawings of pieces of laboratory apparatus made of glass and china. These pieces of apparatus are labelled (a) to (r).

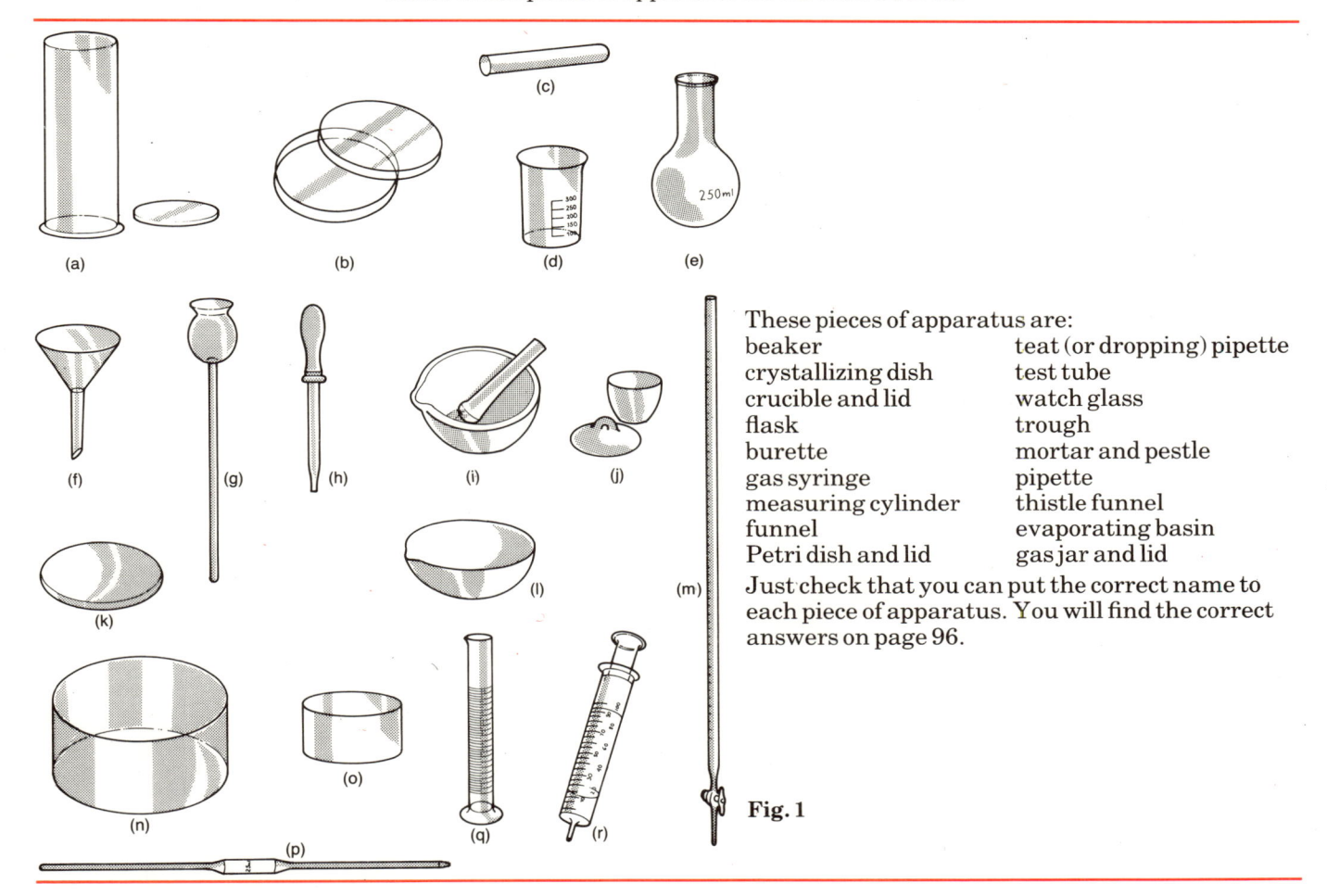

These pieces of apparatus are:

beaker	teat (or dropping) pipette
crystallizing dish	test tube
crucible and lid	watch glass
flask	trough
burette	mortar and pestle
gas syringe	pipette
measuring cylinder	thistle funnel
funnel	evaporating basin
Petri dish and lid	gas jar and lid

Just check that you can put the correct name to each piece of apparatus. You will find the correct answers on page 96.

Fig. 1

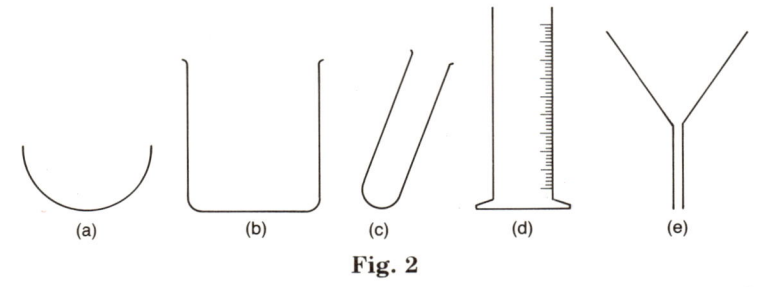

Fig. 2

When we draw diagrams we usually draw **section diagrams**, i.e. what the apparatus would look like if it was cut through the middle from top to bottom. Identify the pieces of apparatus shown in section diagrams in Figure 2. Again you will find the answers on page 96.

The following notes about each piece of apparatus in Figure 1 are designed to help you use them correctly.

89

Fig. 3

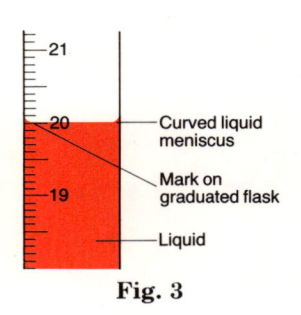

When drawing diagrams of apparatus set up for an experiment, label all pieces of apparatus.

Beaker A general purpose piece of glassware which can be heated. Do not rely on the markings of volume on the side of the beaker as they are very approximate.

Burette A burette is an accurate piece of apparatus used for adding measured volumes of liquid. A burette usually measures volumes to the nearest 0.05 cm^3. The surface of the liquid in the burette is not flat. The curve is called the **meniscus**. When using water or solutions the meniscus goes *down* in the middle and you should always read the bottom of the meniscus (Figure 3).

Crucible and lid These are usually made of glazed china. They are used for more careful heating experiments often involving weighing before and after the experiment.

Crystallizing dish These are made from glass. They are straight-sided. They are used to crystallize solutions.

Evaporating basin An evaporating basin is a china or glass dish used for evaporating solutions.

Flask A flask is another general purpose piece of glassware. It can come in a variety of shapes and sizes. Again any markings on the side of a flask are only approximate. Figure 4 shows a variety of flask shapes drawn as section diagrams. A round-bottomed flask is more suitable for heating than a flat bottomed or conical flask because it is stronger. Can you guess what the divided flask can be used for?

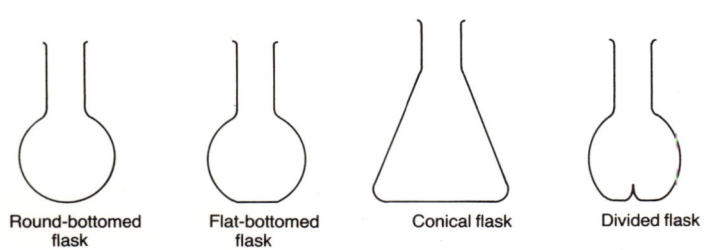

Fig. 4

Funnel A funnel is used widely with a filter paper for filtering (Figure 5). Funnels are also used in other experiments, e.g. in Figure 6.

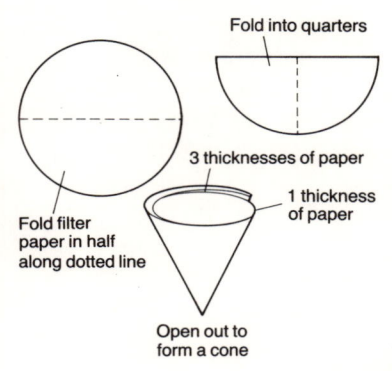

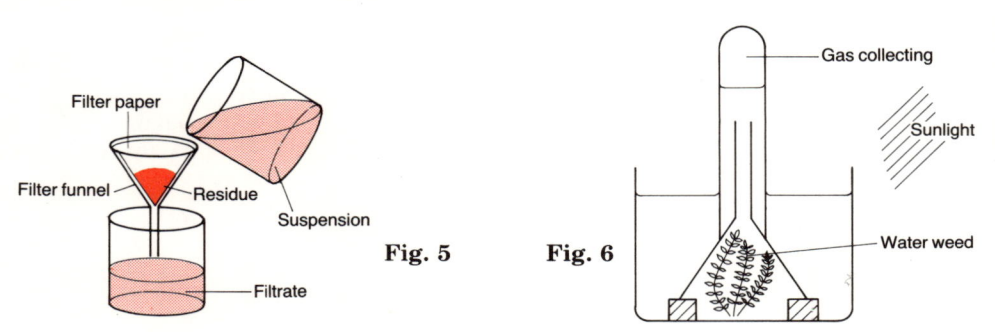

Fig. 5 **Fig. 6**

Gas jar and lid A gas jar is used to collect gases. Figure 7 shows three methods of gas collection. In (a) the gas, for example hydrogen or ammonia, is less dense than air and the method is called **upward delivery**. In (b) the gas, for example sulphur dioxide or hydrogen chloride, is more dense than air. In (c) the gas is collected over water. Before collecting a gas in this way, check to make sure it does *not* dissolve in water.

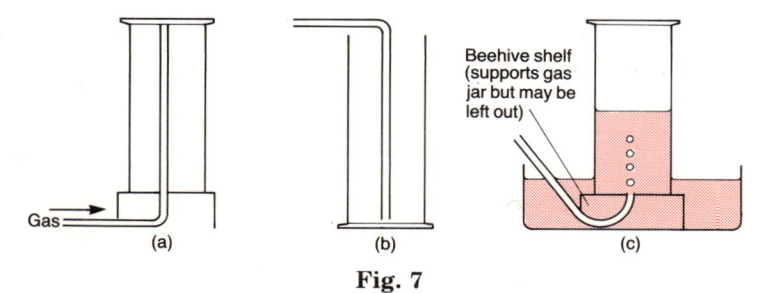

Fig. 7

Gas syringe A gas syringe is used for collecting and measuring the volume of a gas. Plastic syringes are sometimes used to measure out small volumes of liquid.

Measuring cylinder Measuring cylinders are widely used to measure volumes of liquid fairly accurately.

Mortar and pestle These are used for grinding up large lumps into a fine powder. The bowl is the **mortar** and the stick-like grinder is the **pestle**.

Petri dish and lid These are used in microbiological experiments. They must be thoroughly sterilized before and after use. The dish is usually filled with an agar jelly and inoculated with suitable bacteria. Then the lid is put on and the apparatus stored. It is important to store it upside down (Figure 8) to prevent problems caused by condensation.

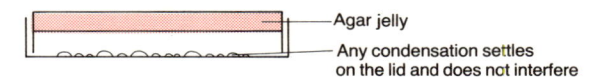

Fig. 8

Pipette A pipette is used to measure out a given volume of liquid accurately. The liquid must be at room temperature. The liquid is sucked up into the pipette with a pipette filler until the bottom of the liquid meniscus is level with the line on the pipette. The liquid is then allowed to drain out. It is possible to get a graduated pipette which has a number of volume markings on it and can be used for measuring out different volumes of liquid.

Teat (or dropping) pipette A piece of apparatus used for adding drops of liquid. It is important to ensure that it is washed out well after use. The liquid should not enter the teat as it causes the teat to rot.

Test tube A test tube is a relatively cheap piece of apparatus which can be used for simple laboratory tests or for heating a substance. Large test tubes are called boiling tubes.

Thistle funnel A thistle funnel is used for adding a liquid to an experiment. If you look at the arrangement of the thistle funnel in the diagrams in Figure 9, (a) is correct and (b) is incorrect. Any gas produced in (b) would escape through the thistle funnel. Sometimes a tap funnel is used for this purpose (Figure 10).

Trough This is a large bowl usually filled with water. It can be used for collecting gases.

Watch glass A watch glass will hold a small volume of solution or a small amount of solid chemical.

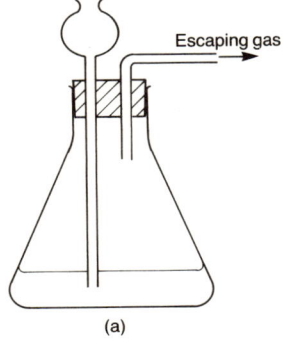

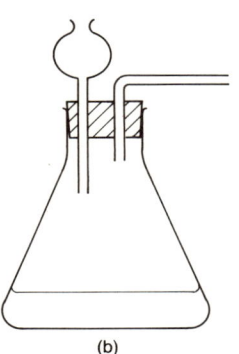

Fig. 9

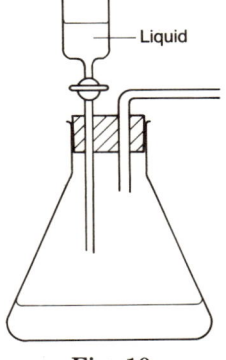

Fig. 10

Other items of general apparatus

Figure 11 shows other pieces of apparatus used in the laboratory. Most of these are made of metal or wood. These pieces of apparatus are labelled (a) to (l).

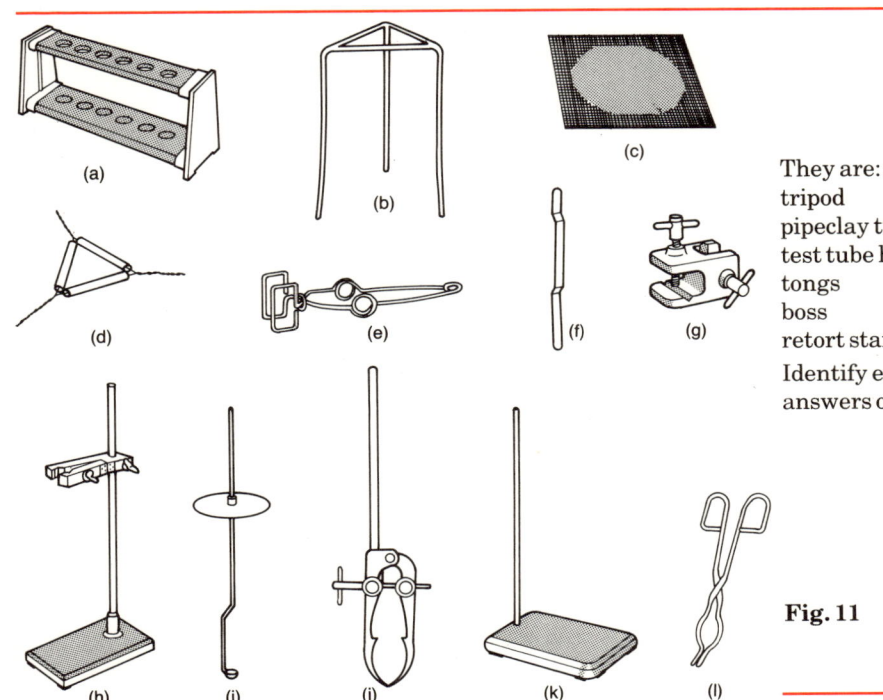

They are:

tripod	gauze
pipeclay triangle	spatula
test tube holders	test tube rack
tongs	combustion spoon
boss	clamp
retort stand	wooden (or burette) stand

Identify each piece of apparatus and check your answers on page 96.

Fig. 11

Fig. 12

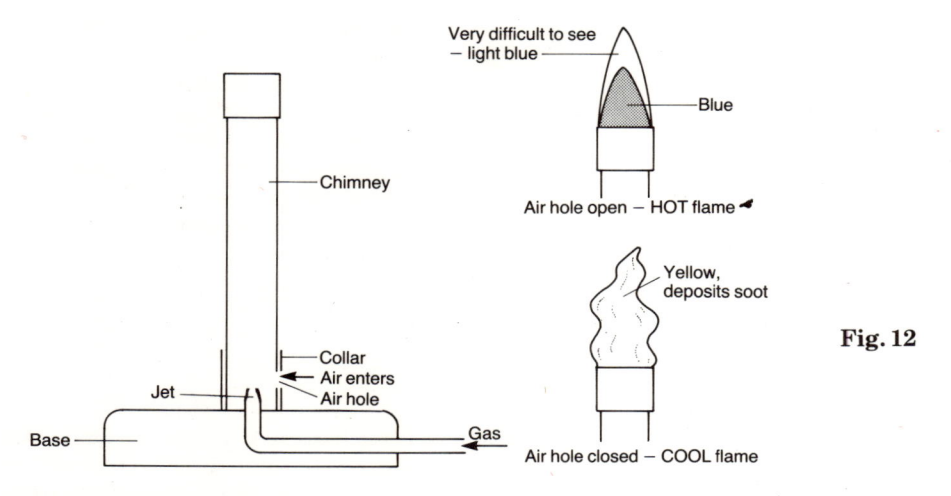

The Bunsen burner

Figure 12 shows a labelled diagram of a Bunsen burner. Turning the collar opens and closes the airhole and alters the flame.

To light a Bunsen burner, turn on the gas supply about half way, turn the collar until the airhole is closed and then apply a lighted splint to the top of the chimney. You should then get a smallish yellow flame. You can then adjust it to suit your requirements.

Weighing equipment

During science lessons you will come across a wide range of instruments for determining weight and mass. The most suitable piece of equipment will vary according to the degree of accuracy that you require. We will consider four types:

- extension spring balance (newtonmeters when used to measure forces)
- compression spring balance
- lever balance
- electronic top pan balance

These are all shown in Figure 13. When using a compression spring balance, lever balance or electronic top pan balance it is important that they stand on a firm and level surface.

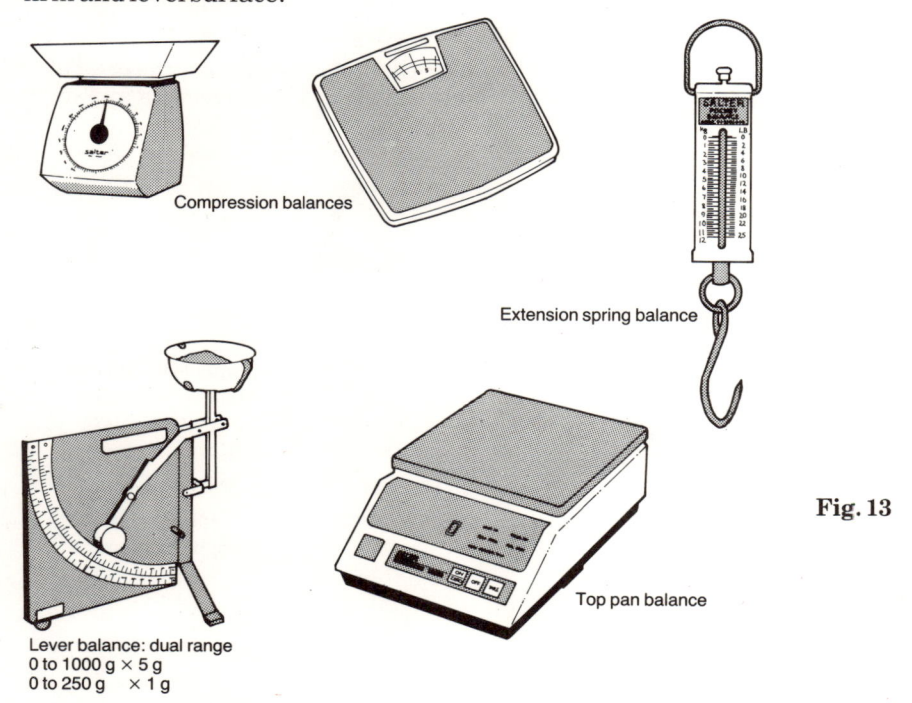

Fig. 13

An **extension spring balance** is used often at a fishing competition to weigh the catch. The object to be weighed is hung on the hook, it extends a spring and the weight can be read off. A balance of this kind is not widely used in science but it can be adapted to read forces directly in newtons. Any reading obtained is very approximate.

A **compression spring balance** works on the opposite principle. When an object is placed on the balance pan it compresses a spring. The amount of compression is registered on a scale. Kitchen scales and bathroom scales are examples of compression spring balances. They are a little more dependable than an extension spring balance.

A **lever balance** is very widely used in science lessons. The object whose mass is to be found is placed on a balance pan and there is a counterweight which balances the object. Usually lever balances are dual scale. The counterweight can be put in two positions and, depending upon the position of the counterweight, one of two scales should be read. The very frequent mistake when using this type of balance is to read the wrong scale.

There is a whole variety of **electronic top pan balances**. They are robust but accurate weighing machines. The usual laboratory machines will weigh to the nearest 0.01 g. It is usually just a matter of plugging them in to an electrical supply, switching on and setting the zero. The objects can be weighed just by placing them on the balance pan. The weighings will either be shown as a digital readout or on some kind of scale. Most balances have a useful **tare** facility. This enables you to put a beaker on the balance pan and arrange for the balance to disregard the mass of the beaker. Then when you add a chemical to the beaker you know exactly how much chemical you have added without having to do subtraction sums. Check if the balance you use has this tare facility and find out how to use it.

Some general points about weighing

1 Never weigh any chemical directly on a balance pan. Use a watch glass or something similar. Apart from the risk of losing some, chemicals can attack the surface of the balance pan.
2 Do not weigh objects hot as they will weigh slightly less.
3 Always make sure that the underside of any container being weighed is dry.
4 Always write down the mass or weight immediately before you have a chance to forget it.

It is possible to link a balance to a computer. This will enable the weighings for example to be directly displayed on a graph or chart.

Fig. 14 A top-pan balance used with a BBC computer

Thermometers

In science you will meet a wide range of thermometers used for measuring temperatures. These will include:

- mercury-in-glass thermometers,
- thermometers producing a digital or scale reading.

Examples of these are shown in Figure 15 and Figure 16.

Mercury-in-glass thermometers are very fragile. Those of the stirring type are slightly more robust. Never put a thermometer near the edge of a bench or sink where it might roll and break. If you break a thermometer, tell your teacher as it is important to clear up the mercury safely. Mercury is very poisonous and gives off a poisonous vapour.

Mercury is poisonous

Alert your teacher if you break a thermometer, so that the poisonous mercury can be cleared up safely.

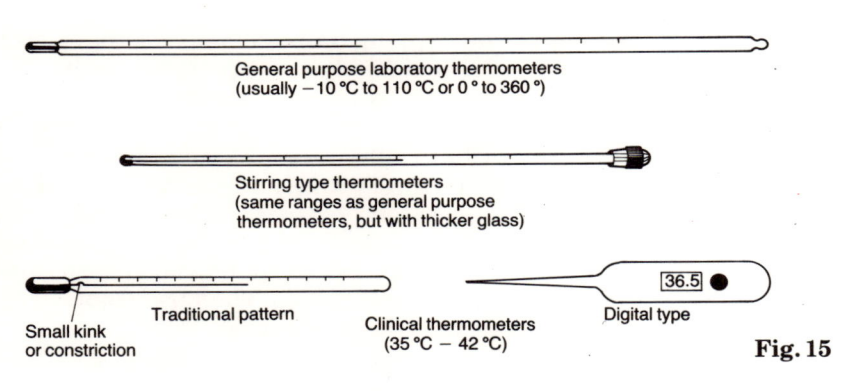

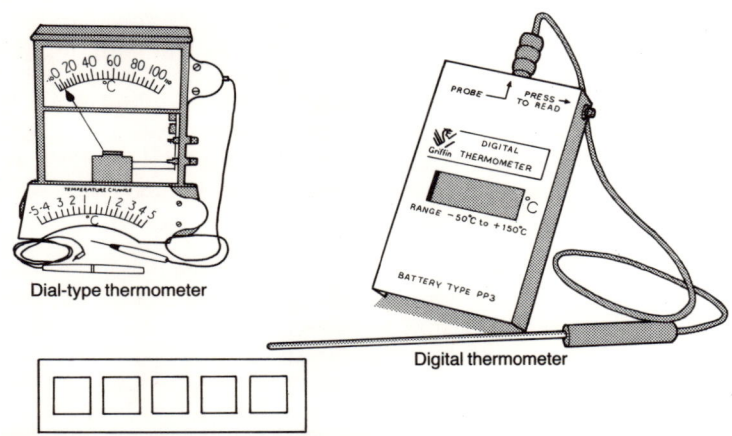

Fig. 15

General purpose laboratory thermometers (usually −10 °C to 110 °C or 0 ° to 360 °)

Stirring type thermometers (same ranges as general purpose thermometers, but with thicker glass)

Traditional pattern — Small kink or constriction

Clinical thermometers (35 °C − 42 °C)

Digital type

Dial-type thermometer

Digital thermometer

Temperature strips — contain liquid crystal and change colour as temperature changes

Fig. 16 Thermometers

When using a thermometer, for example to measure the temperature of a liquid, ensure that the bulb of the thermometer is in the liquid for at least half a minute. Do not lift the thermometer out of the liquid to read the temperature.

Digital or scale thermometers are very easy to use and are specially useful when a series of temperature measurements has to be made.

Electrical apparatus

If you carry out experiments with electricity in science lessons you will inevitably use low voltage. It would be dangerous to use normal electrial supplies. Figure 17 shows one type of transformer used to turn normal voltages (240 V) to a low voltage (perhaps 6 – 12 V). The one illustrated will produce both a.c. (**alternating current**) and d.c. (**direct current**).

Electrical connections may be made with bared wires, with crocodile clips or 4 mm plugs. 4 mm plugs should push into the centre of the terminal (Figure 18). Before connecting bared wires or crocodile clips it is necessary to unscrew the terminal (Figure 19).

A wide variety of measuring instruments are used in electricity experiments. Ammeters measure the electric current, in amps (A) and voltmeters measure the voltage, in volts (V). A selection of ammeters and voltmeters is shown in Figure 20. How can you tell which is which?

The meter labelled A is a **dual scale voltmeter**. You have to work out which scale you should be reading. If the two wires are connected to terminals X and Y the lower scale with a maximum of 5 V has to be used. If the wires are connected to X and Z the upper scale with a maximum of 15 V has to be used.

The current flowing in an electrical circuit can be altered using a **variable resistor** (or **rheostat**). Figure 21 shows two types of variable resistor. A dial type variable resistor is used to alter the volume of a radio or television.

Sometimes, in electrical experiments, after wiring up a circuit you will find it does not work. Check all of the connections first as these may be the cause of the problem. Try replacing any light bulbs.

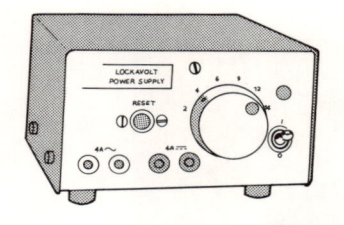

Fig. 17 A transformer

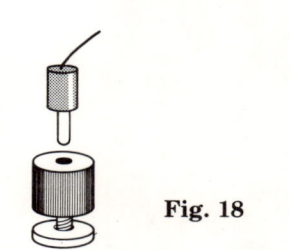

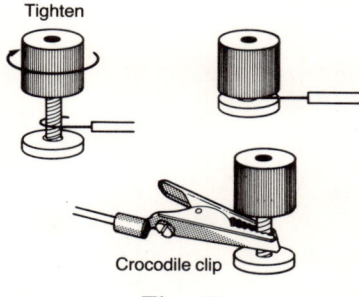

Fig. 18

Fig. 19 Tighten / Crocodile clip

(a) Moving coil voltmeter (b) Moving coil ammeter

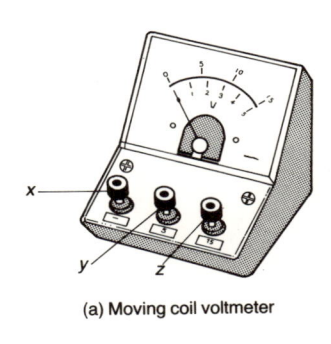

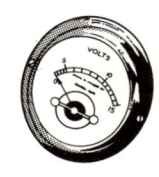

(c) Moving iron voltmeter (d) Moving iron ammeter (e) Digital voltmeter

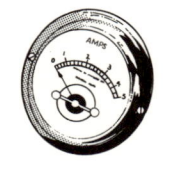

Fig. 20

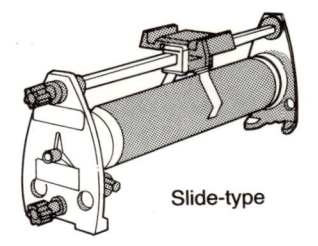

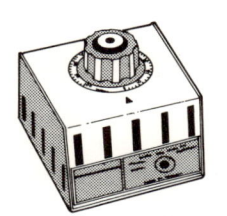

Slide-type

Dial-type

Fig. 21 Variable resistors

Microscopes

In many experiments, especially in biology, you will use a microscope to magnify the object you are looking at. Figure 22 shows a labelled diagram of a **compound microscope**. A compound microscope is a microscope with more than one lens.

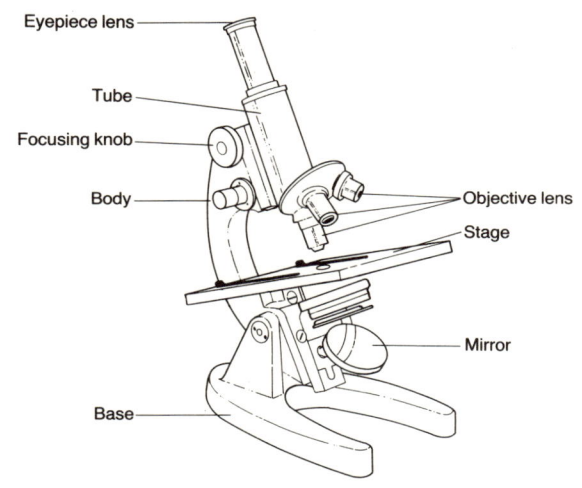

Fig. 22 Parts of a compound microscope

Points to remember when using a microscope

1 Lift the microscope by the body, with the other hand under the base.
2 Put it on a level surface, in a good even light.
3 Turn the focusing knob *a very small amount* to see how it works.
4 Turn the lowest powered objective so that it is directly below the tube. (This is the shortest objective.)
5 Sit or stand behind the body of the microscope so you can look down through the eyepiece in comfort.
6 Look through the eyepiece and move the mirror around until you can see a bright, even light. (Some microscopes have a built-in light and no mirror.)
7 Select an object to be viewed and place it on a microscope slide.
8 Put the microscope slide onto the stage so that the object you want to view is directly below the objective and at the centre of the hole in the stage.
9 Hold your microscope slide in place with the clips.
10 Look at the *side* of the microscope and use the focusing knob to bring the objective and the stage close together.
11 Look down the eyepiece and turn the focusing knob *very slowly towards you*, until the object is sharp and clear.

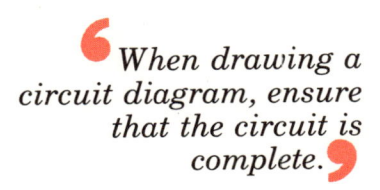

> *When drawing a circuit diagram, ensure that the circuit is complete.*

12 Never look down the microscope and turn the focusing knob away from you. You may crash the objective through the slide.

13 If you need a greater magnification, turn to a higher power (and longer) objective and follow 10 and 11 again.

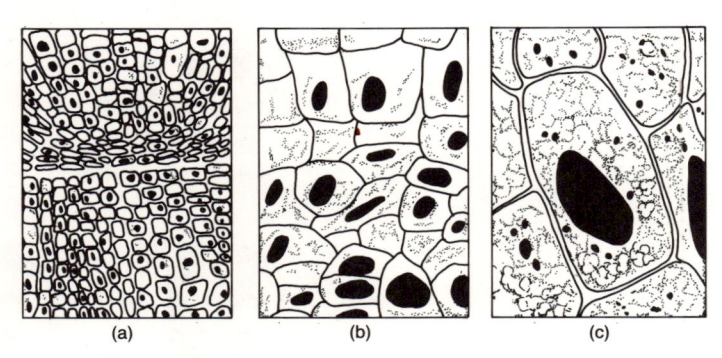

Fig. 23 A plant root at different magnifications

Figure 23 shows the change that can be brought about varying the objective and hence the magnification. Part (a) shows a plant root through a low power microscope. Each little 'brick' is a plant cell. In (b) and (c) the same sample is looked at with increasing magnification. The detail in the cells can be seen clearly.

An **electron microscope** is a most complicated microscope. The image is displayed on a television screen. It can give much greater magnification.

Centrifuge

A centrifuge is used to separate solid particles from a liquid. It could be used to separate a precipitate from a solution.

When using a centrifuge, balance the sample test tube with one containing an equal volume of water.

Then switch the centrifuge on for about half a minute. The central spindle rotates at very high speed and the test tubes move out horizontally (Figure 24). Solid particles settle at the bottom of the test tube. The liquid can be removed from above the solid with a teat pipette.

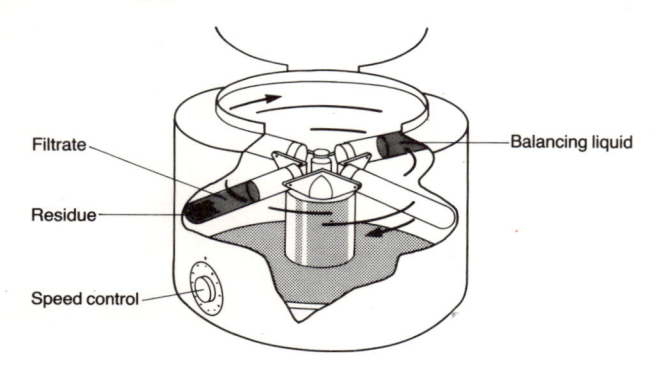

Fig. 24 A centrifuge in operation

Answers

Figure 1 (a) gas jar and lid; (b) Petri dish and lid; (c) test tube; (d) beaker; (e) flask; (f) funnel; (g) thistle funnel; (h) teat pipette; (i) mortar and pestle; (j) crucible and lid; (k) watch glass; (l) evaporating basin; (m) burette; (n) trough; (o) crystallizing dish; (p) pipette; (q) measuring cylinder; (r) gas syringe.

Figure 2 (a) evaporating basin; (b) beaker; (c) test tube; (d) measuring cylinder; (e) funnel

Figure 3 A divided flask is useful when two reacting substances need to be kept apart. The reaction only starts when the flask is shaken and the substances mix.

Figure 11 (a) test tube rack; (b) tripod; (c) gauze; (d) pipeclay triangle; (e) test tube holder; (f) spatula; (g) boss; (h) wooden stand; (i) combustion spoon; (j) clamp; (k) retort stand; (l) tongs